MW01193485

DATA, STRATEGY, CULTURE & POWER

DATA, STRATEGY, CULTURE & POWER

Win with Data-Centric AI by
making human nature work for you

N. M. Radziwill

Data, Strategy, Culture & Power

© 2024 by N. M. Radziwill

All rights reserved. Printed in the United States of America

ISBN-13: 978-0-9969160-8-0
Library of Congress Control Number: 2024909830

Cover Design:	Morgan C. Benton
Publisher:	Lapis Lucera
	Pittsburgh, PA

First Edition
May 27, 2024

For the free PDF eBook, please send a copy of your receipt to books@qzuku.com with "DSCP PDF" in the subject line.

XKCD comics by Randal Munroe (http://xkcd.com) are included under the terms of the Creative Commons Attribution-NonCommercial 2.5 License. (More information at https://xkcd.com/license.html). The information contained within this book is distributed without warranty. While author, copyeditors, and publisher have taken every precaution to assure quality and correctness, they assume no responsibility or liability for errors, omissions, or damages caused directly or indirectly by the information contained within it.

*This book is for everyone who shares the goals
Tom Peters outlined in* Extreme Humanism *(2021),
especially this one:*

*Never again: "Best companies to work for."
Hereinafter: "**Healthiest** companies to work for."*

*Healthiest companies to work for foster radical employee
growth and exceptional engagement within their
communities, offer products and services
aimed at making the world a bit better, and are
demonstrable paragons of integrity.*

TABLE OF CONTENTS

"Radziwill's Law"

*"Data cannot be decoupled from power.
Organizations create and use data, analytics, and AI
in ways that embed and reflect
the **power structures and power differentials** between
the people that develop and use them over time."*

All data, analytics, and AI output will encapsulate the power structures and dynamics between the people and groups that *originally* developed them *and* the ones that use them, *no matter how far in the future that use occurs*. How an organization is structured, how teams are formed, and how power is distributed will heavily influence the utility of a data-driven system. Key implications are:

1.   An organization with hierarchical or imbalanced power structures, not fully conscious of its own biases, will produce data-driven insights that perpetuate or amplify those power differentials. (Note: this is *all of us*.)

2.   Creating trustworthy data-driven systems first requires establishing trust between *people*.

3.   Changes in organizational power dynamics will result in changes in how data, analytics, and AI are produced or used.

4.   Understanding an organization's power structures can help uncover limitations of the data, analytics, and AI it produces and the actions it takes as a result.

Power dynamics and organizational factors are just as critical as technical considerations while designing and developing data-driven systems. These systems can also extend *well beyond* the people and purpose they were originally created for. To win with Data-Centric AI, account for power differentials in data-driven decision-making processes.

Data

The signs and signals that deceive and inform, bringing _knowledge_, revealing where we _can_ go, helping us decide where we _want_ to go, and finding paths that will help us get there

Strategy

The business _systems_ we are embedded within, the goals we choose, the rationale behind the decisions we make, and the ways we leverage people, processes & technology to achieve our goals

Culture

The expectations we set and reinforce for standards of behavior and performance; the _variation_ in _who we are_ and how we interact with one another day to day; how we use data and wield personal power

Power

The _psychology_ of trauma and the conditions that drive emotion, action, and inspiration; the ubiquitous effects of human nature (good and bad); the illusions that compel behavior and influence

PREFACE

"Power tends to corrupt, and absolute power corrupts absolutely. Great men are almost always bad men, even when they exercise influence and not authority. There is no worse heresy than that the office that sanctifies the holder of it."
-- Lord Acton, English writer and politician (1834-1902)

Most people start thinking about power only when they feel *utterly powerless.* When the math doesn't math, or egos won't budge. Or when reality breaks down and reveals that **people will do most anything to uphold paycheck-producing illusions.**

Five years ago, I started this journey. *Do I need power? Can't I just lead through inspiration and influence?* I had, to that point, resisted claiming *any* power, choosing instead to double down on empowering others. Early in my life, especially at one private school, I was taught that powerful people are oftentimes bad, that power can corrupt, and that power dynamics between people yield unbalanced and unhealthy relationships. Power did not seem to be something *any* good person should pursue. I didn't want to *have* to dominate others, and I certainly didn't want to be a bad person.

But the *lack* of power, I noticed, could often be the root of distress. Without *power*, it's hard to get anything accomplished. Without *empowerment*, it's difficult to get the social support that brings power. Lack of empowerment tends to lead to dissatisfaction and loneliness at work.

I've spent the past two decades working with data, analytics, AI and software teams. These groups often feel disempowered and despondent. The volume of work these teams are expected to shoulder is extreme, and they are constantly asked to prove their value. Job satisfaction, stress, burnout, and retention issues are ubiquitous among these populations, from the smallest startups to the largest enterprises.

THE POWER OF CULTURE

For our organizations to thrive with artificial intelligence (AI), we must do better: **it's the power of the people *behind* the AI that determines whether we collectively succeed or fail.** People are *remarkably flawed and even more variable*, even under the best of conditions. Statistically, in a 100-person company, 18 people will have anxiety and 9 people will experience depression. Up to 5 people will be sociopaths, predisposed to emotional volatility, and will find it difficult to maintain relationships. One or two people will be psychopaths, void of true emotion or empathy. And just *lacking* empathy does not mean they won't pretend – often very *convincingly* – that they *do* have it.

We tend to pretend these harsher dynamics don't exist, or that our coworkers can have their egos and bad behavior *trained* out of them. But egos and conflicts are unavoidable, and behavior that's "bad" to one person might be perfectly acceptable to another. Culture is defined by core values and inspirational adages that are rarely implemented uniformly in practice, and that, in extreme cases, can be weaponized by devious coworkers.

According to John Cutler, expert and thought leader in product management, company culture is more than the words you use to describe it. Here is a broad list of factors he shared on LinkedIn that are key to company culture(paraphrased):

- What you say, and how often you say it
- What, when, and how you celebrate
- The losses and missteps you acknowledge, and how you respond to them

- How you behave when the chips are down
- What you fight for at all costs
- The corners you cut
- Who you hire, promote, compensate, and fire
- Who you "smoke out" until they leave the organization
- The worst behavior you accept and the best behavior you reject
- The voices you amplify, and the voices you suppress
- When you encourage conformity, and when you promote diversity
- How you handle disagreements and differences
- How and where you spend your time and money
- What gets discussed at the water cooler
- What gets discussed out in the open and what is shared behind closed doors
- The contradictions you allow vs. the ones you stamp out
- The exceptions you make vs. things that never budge
- Who sits together and how you arrange your office
- Who gets access to the best tools, technology, and infrastructure and who has to wait
- What you say about your customers during challenging situations

All these elements of culture will reinforce power differentials for good or ill. They can shift power structures towards inclusive collaboration or entrench coercion and control. This book, based on research in inclusion and performance, was written to help you navigate the complexities of power around data, analytics, and AI. Healthy power can be good, but unhealthy power can ingrain powerlessness., making it difficult to work with joy.

Lack of the feeling of control can lead to melancholy and depression, both at work and in life. It can compel good people to lash out, to become violent, or even to descend into collective madness. These are all outcomes most of us would like to resist.

MAL DE MORZINE

The mid-19th century was a time of significant upheaval in France. The country was still grappling with the effects of the 1848 revolution, which saw the overthrow of the monarchy and the establishment of the French Second Republic. In the rural and isolated areas like Morzine in the French Alps, just one mountain away from the Swiss border, political instability was exacerbated by social and economic challenges. Agricultural failures, poor harvests, and a lack of industrial development left many in extreme poverty.

As conditions became more and more difficult, by 1857 more than half of the younger men were spending several months of the year away, providing labor in larger cities like Geneva and Lausanne. Up to this point, gender roles had been rigidly defined, with women confined to the domestic sphere. But without men to provide labor locally, workloads had to shift to ensure survival. For women and girls in particular, responsibilities became even more extreme, options for self-determination were severely limited, and prospects for acceptable marriages were diminishing as men brought back mates from the cities.

The powerlessness that women and girls experienced as the social balance was upended was often profound. With limited access to education and largely excluded from decision-making, they had no choice but to maintain the status quo. The social pressure to unswervingly adhere to the strict moral codes of Catholicism that elevated them above their secular Swiss neighbors placed further constraints on their behavior, requiring obedience, humility, and modesty. Any deviation from the norm, including illness or distress, could be interpreted as a sign of personal, moral, or spiritual failure.

Lacking other means to express their distress or challenge their circumstances, a mysterious "demonic possession" began to infect women and girls of Morzine. Seizures, trances, strange voices, and convulsions offered a way to communicate suffering and attract attention to their plight. Moreover, the language of possession, so deeply embedded in the cultural and religious narratives of the time (and particularly in this devout village), provided a framework for understanding and articulating these otherwise inexpressible experiences. The series of events came to be known as the "Mal de Morzine" and can be seen as a manifestation of the deep-seated anxieties, frustrations, and powerlessness of those who were suffering.

Resolving the situation was not straightforward. The Catholic Church, initially supporting the demonic possession narrative, performed numerous exorcisms. They didn't alleviate any of the symptoms, but they *did* remove all hope and trust in Morzine's priests. The French government, with the intention to undermine the influence of the Vatican, considered the events evidence of the church's negative influence.

The environment was saturated with hidden enemies and was ripe for betrayals. Leaders sent in Adolphe Constans, psychiatrist and head inspector for France's asylums, to restore order. While he achieved some success by moving afflicted people to hospitals in larger towns, and by expanding their contact with nearby communities, locals were aware that some women continued expressing symptoms of possession (in private) for two more decades. (Harris, 1997)

While this story helps us see how people can react desperately to systemic and ever-deepening feelings of powerlessness, it also reveals insights about the connections between data, strategy, culture, and power.

*"The language of the possessed
enables us to listen to the muted voices."*
-- Ruth Harris *in* Possession on the Borders

Where's the data in this situation? It's *everywhere*: people collect "impressions" of situations and others around them all the time, regardless of whether this "data" is formally gathered.

In Morzine, we see several potential independent variables (the symptoms and their durations and moments of onset; the physical, social, and emotional characteristics of the women and girls; their past personal experiences). We've got the dependent variables that we're most interested in predicting (whether an individual is "possessed"; the time an individual will recover; the time until the entire village is recovered). Their degree of satisfaction or dissatisfaction with their lives could be either independent or dependent, depending upon the intentions of whoever is trying to understand the situation or choose interventions. If you're a data scientist or a statistician, you'll immediately start seeing a survival model emerge, and you'll already be thinking about censoring (not the political kind).

There were two strategies applied in this situation by the Vatican and the French government, each directed towards the shared goal of ending the outbreak. The Vatican sent priests to Morzine to conduct more exorcisms. The French government sent an inspector from psychiatric institutions to specifically address the root causes and the displays of mental illness. (Hewitt, 2020)

Both were valid approaches given the intensely devout culture of the village, in which *belief could be manipulated*, and the political power that the government granted the inspector. Because the inspector was able to remove people from the village, provide emotional supporters to help other sufferers genuinely recover, and drive the rest that could not recover into hiding... his political power and reputation were reinforced.

DATA, STRATEGY, CULTURE & POWER

Data provides the information (and confidence) that helps us formulate and select goal-directed strategies, both personally and professionally. Those strategies require a receptive culture to take root and grow. If one is present, the power to act is enabled. If the culture is conducive to it, the power of collective action is *also* released. Personal power comes from the ability to leverage collective action to get results, and to control the variety, accessibility, and flow of data and information. Control over information limits the strategies that can be discovered.

BIG DATA IS A BIG DISTRACTION

"Data is the new oil" became a tired and irrelevant cliche in the 2010s (and maybe even earlier). While the analogy may have been useful to raise some people's awareness of the value of data, it oversimplifies the complexities and the potential of capturing, curating, and using data intelligently. Data is not a finite resource that can be extracted and depleted; it is a dynamic and ever-expanding asset, subject to entropy and constant degradation (even when it's sitting unused).

In contrast, data is more like electricity: a utility that the business stakeholders who *use* data expect to turn on and *just work*. They don't care about the difficulty or complexity of delivering that electricity, they just want to be able to flip the switch. And so it is with data, still decades away from performing like a utility. In the meantime, those stakeholders hold the power position, unconvinced that their expectations are unreasonable.

Data encapsulates a universe of potential energy waiting to be unleashed. The key to awakening this dormant force lies not within the data itself, but in the beliefs and inspirations it fuels, that compel us to act.

Yet, in the face of this immense opportunity, many business and technology leaders find themselves lost in a sea of information, drowning in a deluge of data that threatens to overwhelm everyone. They've spent time and money making sure *all* the data is captured, not stopping to reflect on *whether* that data has meaning or potential value. By mistakenly focusing on the mythical power of the data itself, it's easy to lose sight of where the true power lies: in our ability to manage and harness the *effects* data has on *behavior*.

The focus, then, should not be on accumulating data, but on gathering, curating, and applying data in ways that will unleash action in the desired directions. Viewing data solely as a commodity fails to capture its *potentially* transformative power, and de-emphasizes the need for organizations to consciously (and continuously!) pay attention to building a data-driven culture that will truly harness its potential.

UNIFYING THEMES

Data, Strategy, Culture, and Power will help you see how data, analytics, and AI shapes and shifts the power dynamics between anyone who creates or uses data. Reading this book will help you intentionally engineer the work systems that underpin return on investment, especially for AI. Written for current and emerging leaders in business and technology, this book is a guide for leveraging data as a source of power. There are four key themes, supported by stories and analogies drawn from history, art, entertainment, and business:

Seeing Beyond the Data to its Purpose. Too often, organ
fall into the trap of data obsession, believing that accum
vast amounts of information is the key to success. (After
more information you have, the more likely you can make c ᴗᴗse
for any outcome you want.) This book challenges the lure of data,
encouraging leaders to see beyond the tantalizing mirage of
"bigger is better" to focus on the strategic implications and
possibilities that data holds. (People are starting to become
conscious of this. Google Trends, as of early 2023, shows that
interest and enthusiasm in Big Data began to surge in 2012,
peaked in 2014 and 2015, and has been slowly and gradually
losing traction ever since.)

Strategy as the Driving Force. Effective data management
requires a well-defined strategy that aligns with the
organization's goals and objectives. How do you know if your data
strategy is aligned? It's not a simple or straightforward question
to answer. This book explores the critical components of data
strategy, offering approaches to develop and validate a robust
data strategy that will empower the right people leaders to make
the decisions that will shape the future direction of their
organizations.

Culture as a Catalyst. The book highlights the importance of
fostering a culture that embraces data and analytics, enabling
employees at all levels to become active participants in the data
journey. Most significantly, we highlight the roles that power
dynamics and interpersonal gamesmanship play, two factors
that invariably arise when people struggle to maintain their
status and livelihood under pressure. No company is completely
psychologically healthy, just as no person is fully content and
satisfied all the time. Rather than trying to train the variation out
of people, we acknowledge the immutability of variation and seek
to work *with* it.

Power through Effective Data Management: The true power of data lies not in accumulating data in data warehouses or data lakes but in managing, using, and curating it effectively. This book draws from research dating back to the 1980s and 1990s to reveal elements of successful data management practices, including data quality, integration, and governance. It adapts those lessons to the present time and the emerging future, anticipating how artificial intelligence and machine learning will be leveraged to optimize data processes and extract actionable insights. By taking an 80/20 approach to the art of data management (that is, learning how to identify the 20% of the work that unlocks 80% of the business value) leaders can unlock the full potential of their data assets and *actually* gain a competitive advantage in the market, rather than just talking about it.

The stories in this book will help raise your awareness of how power differentials impact how we create and use data, and how relationships change in the process. This audience includes anyone who works *in* data (data analysts, business intelligence specialists, data scientists, and Directors, VPs, and Chief Data and Analytics Officers, Chief AI Officers) and anyone who works *with* data (business analysts, line managers, sales executives, heads of marketing, heads of product). If you've been feeling powerless, this book was written to help you begin uncovering the root cause of that feeling so you can take conscious action to address it.

Whether you want to feel *more powerful or less powerless*, this book encourages you to explore which threads you can pull on to get what you want or need. Like jedi training, it will be possible to misuse these lessons, becoming a force of the dark side that uses data to manipulate rather than illuminate. Choose wisely.

DO YOU NEED POWER?

Yes. Everyone needs power. The right kind of power (at the right time) can mean the difference between achievement and failure, between vibrance and despondency, and between supporting others *fully* - or letting them down.

This book will help you see power differentials and begin to use them to your advantage... while generating *even more power* to call everyone around you to action. By learning how to use data to harness the power latent in the people and systems around you, and to avoid (or change) the situations that drain power from you and your organization, you can create a data strategy that stands the test of time.

> *"You never change things by fighting the existing reality. To change something, build a new model that makes the existing model obsolete."*
> — Buckminster Fuller

While there are many excellent references that focus on human bias and how it seeps into training machine learning models, this book chooses a different emphasis. It explores forces *within you* and your organization that can threaten the success of your data, analytics, AI or data-using business units.

Data, Strategy, Culture & Power presents the *ultimate recipe for sustainable data strategy* as you participate in the collective sport of transforming data into true intelligence. Data & AI can empower and liberate *or* be used to coerce and confuse. The choice is now yours.

REFERENCES

Harris, R. (1997). Possession on the Borders: The "Mal de Morzine" in Nineteenth-Century France. *Journal of Modern History*, 69(3), 451-478.

Hewitt, J. (2020). Institutionalizing Gender: Madness, the Family, and Psychiatric Power in Nineteenth-Century France (p. 264). Cornell University Press.

PART I:

NAVIGATING THE PITFALLS OF PERCEPTION

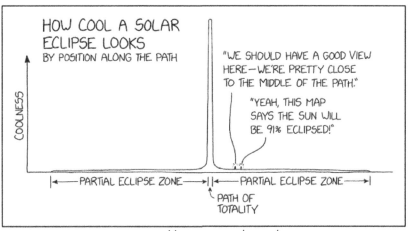

https://xkcd.com/2914/

CHAPTER 1

BEWARE OF THE LIMITS OF TRUTH

*"A man with a conviction is a hard man to change. Tell him you disagree
and he turns away. Show him facts or figures and he questions your
sources. Appeal to logic and he fails to see your point."*
*- Leon Festinger, psychologist who originated the term "cognitive
dissonance" in* When Prophecy Fails *(1957)*

Before the growth and expansion of railroads on the American frontier, there really wasn't a need for accurate, shared timekeeping on the scale of the entire country. "Noon" just described the moment when the sun was high in the sky, at the zenith, and most towns displayed a clock in their center that matched this physical phenomenon, at least approximately. Using the community clock, people could synchronize their watches, and coordinate their daily lives (which weren't intricately connected or global, like ours are today).

But not every train used the same town as its sole source of truth for time. This led to unfortunate consequences for travelers hoping to make their connection to another train or railway line. By 1883, the situation had become uncomfortable enough that the railroads decided to act.

Together, they agreed to coordinate their timekeeping by introducing time zones and standardizing measurement of noon to a particular location within that zone. This meant that in Indianapolis, for example, the sun would now reach its zenith at 12:16pm. This so outraged some of the locals that they published editorials and opinions in the newspaper calling for immediate return to "God's Time." (IndyStar, 2018) God, however, did not comment, and over the next decade time zones became more broadly accepted.

By 1949, another skirmish over time measurement had erupted in Indiana, putting business owners and farmers at odds. Most business owners wanted to be in the same time zone as New York City, to make it easier to do business with larger, more established firms. Other business owners claimed that it made more sense to align with the time zone in Chicago, since more business opportunities naturally came from that area. Farmers were not interested in adopting complex clock time agreements at all, as it was believed to be "unhealthy for cows". When a bill was introduced in the state senate to outlaw daylight saving time and standardize on Central time all year round, some legislators were angry. They filibustered, confusing participants by manipulating the hands on the official clock so much that they broke, and the session didn't end until just before sunrise. (Moser, 2012)

The King: "Where do I set the hands of the clock?"
The Scientist: "Oh, that…
you can set them any place you want."
-- From "About Time",
Bell System Science Series, by Bell Labs (1962)

To this day, the practice of changing the clocks can stir up strong emotions. The energy savings that were so often claimed to be the primary benefit of the time change haven't stood up to statistical scrutiny over the years. Health magazines often publish articles in November noting that the time change is associated with increased seasonal affective disorder, decreased motivation at work, and the disruption of morning activities. (Wade, 2021) More in-depth investigations by academic researchers have indeed suggested an increased incidence of car accidents, heart attacks, workplace injuries, and even a decrease in life satisfaction. (Costa-Font et al., 2021)

But these problems might not emerge from the inherent goodness of one time scheme or another, but from going through the motions of changing the clocks and failing to account for statistical covariates (like the increased incidence of traffic accidents at night as compared to the daytime). Standardizing on daylight saving time would "make our lives sunnier" by adding 366 brighter hours to the time most people spend awake, some claim. (Nosowitz, 2022) Others point to the fact that the U.S. already tried once, making daylight saving time permanent between January and October of 1974 to mitigate an energy crisis brought on by an oil embargo from the Organization of Arab Petroleum Exporting Countries. Although the move saved 2% of the country's oil consumption over that winter season, there were many reports of people disgruntled by the unyielding four-month morning darkness. (Shammas, 2022)

It seems that this may be the single issue that makes bipartisan tension melt away. On March 15, 2022, the United States Senate passed a bill, the "Sunshine Protection Act," to make Daylight Saving Time *permanent*. The bill would make the practice of shifting clocks twice a year archaic by standardizing on summer time, and keeping it year round. Most residents of the country have been *"springing forward and falling back"* their entire lives, turning the clocks back an hour each fall and an extra hour ahead each spring, and most everyone has (at some point) inadvertently shown up early or late the next day to school, to work, or to meetings. With the advent of geolocated mobile phones, this pain has largely been ameliorated: even if *you* don't remember the time change, *your phone will*. But with all this regulatory attention focused on the policy for timekeeping and time changes, another problem has come to light (no pun intended).

THE PROBLEM OF AMBIGUITY

It turns out that nobody knows *exactly* where the boundaries for time zones *are*.

> *"A person may take knowing the local time for granted,*
> *but an official review revealed that **there is no single,**
> ***accurate map showing the nation's time zones***
> *and local observance of Daylight Saving Time."*
> *-- Gregory Wallace in CNN Politics Blog (9/22/2022)*

The official boundaries are described in terms of state lines, county lines, and geographic features like rivers, with descriptions that are both unclear and outdated in places. There are also noteworthy discrepancies, particularly around Elko in northeastern Nevada. "Investigators found no single map accurately showing the boundaries nationwide and said several sources of time information on the DOT website contained errors, such as inaccurately noting the time practices in some localities." (Wallace, 2022) Unofficial boundaries are the ones used by the cell phone companies who leverage telephony time zone detection. In Europe, this works using signals from the Network Identity and Time Zone (NITZ), which is dictated by the Global System for Mobile Communications (GSM) standard.

The U.S. Department of Transportation (USDOT) is *supposed* to be the authority for exact time zone boundaries for all states. Since the halcyon days of the frontier railroads, they have been responsible for evaluating and establishing the time zone assignments that best support commerce. They receive petitions to change time zones, and apply the "convenience of commerce" heuristics required by the Uniform Time Act of 1966. There are two problems: first, petitions are only received once every few decades, so processing petitions is not part of workforce training.

Second, the department has not kept records describing how petitions are interpreted, reviewed, and evaluated.

It's kind of like when you have that important dashboard or database driving a key business process, but the person who built and maintained it left a couple years ago and no one quite knows how it works. "As a result, DOT cannot have reasonable assurance that the information used to evaluate the impact of future time zone changes will be the best and most relevant evidence and data, as required by current rulemaking procedures. If DOT does not ensure its decisions are based on high-quality data, time zone changes may have unanticipated negative effects on residents and businesses in the affected area." (USDOT, 2022)

Before the government can officially change the time zones in its territory, it needs to know exactly what the boundaries of those time zones are. So in preparation for the country's potential shift to all daylight time all the time, the USDOT has set out to map out the details of its time zones once and for all.

And then everyone will be content. Right?

THE EVOLUTION OF TRUTH

If you're a professional software engineer, you know exactly how miserable it is to work with times and time zones, and the contribution that the mosaic of daylight saving time laws have made to your misery. (It's even impacted my self-knowledge: I was born just a few hours after *spring forward*, a piece of trivia I didn't know until I was in my late 20s... meaning I'm a little more of an early bird than I originally thought.)

Regardless of the languages you program in, or the operating systems you depend on, there's one utility that you can't live without (whether you know it or not): tzdb, the time zone database. Founded by Arthur Olsen at the National Institutes of Health (NIH) in the early 1980s, the project was adopted by Paul Eggert, a lecturer at the UCLA Samueli School of Engineering, and is carefully maintained by a group of dedicated volunteers. All Linux and Mac machines use this reference data, which captures all historical time zone designations and all civil changes since 1970 (the "beginning of the world", in Unix time).

Maintaining tzdb is a complex undertaking for several reasons. First, it's not just important to know how to look up the time zone for the locale associated with your computer or mobile device right now, but also to be able to reference data measured at points in time using the appropriate time zone designation. Financial transactions, weather data, and times of birth and death recorded by departments of health are just a few examples of historical records that are sensitive to accurate time zone knowledge. Consequently, this resource has grown into one of the most comprehensive historical records of time zone evolution by locale.

Second, data like this can be a source of geopolitical advantage or disadvantage. "What makes the thankless task for Eggert and a small team of IANA 'zone keepers' even more complicated is geopolitics. That's when governments sometimes decide to change their time zones unilaterally with just a few days' notice. Time becomes currency for these governments looking to flex their political muscles and alter the time without properly alerting the rest of the world." (UCLA, 2022) I remember something similar happening when I showed up for work at a weather research lab on Thursday, March 25, 1999, where we were building a network of new weather instrumentation using GPS signals. Overnight, all our raw data had been injected with offsets, making our analysis faulty. To facilitate the bombing of Serbian military positions in the Yugoslavian province of Kosovo, someone, somewhere, had turned off the high precision positioning capabilities we typically had access to.

Third, decisions about how a society should engage in timekeeping are often made in a highly distributed way. For example, even though Arizona (as a state) has made the legislative decision to follow Mountain Standard Time and *not* spring forward into daylight saving time each year, the Navajo Nation *does* observe the time change.

Because of all these factors, building a source of truth for time zones is a continuous, iterative effort, more like the historical reconstruction an archaeologist might work on than a data management project. The database is updated as new, verifiable information is received that changes the maintainers' understanding of one part of the historical record. It's similar to the process of building archives of weather or ecological data, which has historically been gathered by multiple sources of variable (and sometimes unknown) quality. Obtaining new information that agrees with old information strengthens confidence in the old information, and obtaining new information that contradicts old information reduces confidence. Over time, a trustworthy reference is constructed.

But managing the evolution of `tzdb` is different, too, in one *very* critical way.

THE POWER OF PRESENCE

"The codebase itself is no problem, [Eggert] said, but the interests of various parties can muddy the waters and make the work unexpectedly contentious." (UCLA, 2022) There are at least five categories of participants in this political dance in the U.S. alone:

- The federal government
- State, local, and tribal governments
- The USDOT
- Phone companies
- The IANA/ICANN
- Standards organizations, like the European Telecommunications Standards Institute (ETSI) that manages the GSM standard

Who gets to decide exactly which time zone a locale adheres to? Who gets to share and disseminate the information? Both play a role in the provenance of truth. For example, if the decider and the disseminator disagree, who has more power to influence people regarding what reference they use? What if there's a conflict about who gets to be the decider? "Taking sides" by making an executive decision about what gets stored in the shared database can put unbiased tech people in the line of fire... sometimes literally.

This is precisely the case in the current geopolitical hotspot of Ukraine and Crimea: "... if you go to Crimea and try to configure your Unix-based system to the local time, you'll see an indication in the interface that you're in Russia, which understandably pisses off Ukrainians and is not in line with what most governments think. You can check this out on some time zone web sites. The services at time.is and timeanddate.com both refer to Europe/Simferopol as being in Ukraine, while WorldTimeServer says it's in Russia." (Murphy, 2019) The head of the Cyberpolice Department of the National Police of Ukraine has even threatened legal action. But removal of Russia would undoubtedly lead to backlash from the other side. Eggert has proposed a compromise where for the period of the dispute, parts of the region will be listed under both countries.

It's not a perfect compromise, and will certainly have longer-term implications for historical time series gathered during this time. But it's enough to keep lawsuits away and guns pointed in other directions, which will help ensure the continuity of `tzdb` operations. Accurately measuring and recording time requires global collaboration and coordination, even when people are not motivated to participate (or, conversely, are motivated to participate in ways that achieve their *own* geopolitical ends). According to Eggert, this will be the greatest challenge facing the `tzdb` project for decades to come.

In practice, what determines time zone reality is what the *people* in a locale believe and enact. Which time zone governs their experience of life every day (or do they still abide by "God's Time")? How do people in the rest of the world engage them in personal and professional transactions? And how can we make sure future generations get an accurate picture of what their reality was?

THE GHOSTS IN THE ARCHIVE

To find out, we can look to the experiences of historical researchers who have been faced with the challenge of interacting with archives that have been built under political pressure. Tesar (2015), for example, shares his experiences as an archival researcher after the Velvet Revolution of 1989. "As children growing up in communist Czechoslovakia," he reports, "we had developed a complex relationship with truth." This relationship was shattered upon the fall of the Iron Curtain, when he and others who had grown up during that time found that "almost all that we had learnt and acquired as knowledge was suddenly proclaimed to be false."

Under the totalitarian government and the ubiquitous presence of the secret police, "each and every citizen became both a supporter and a victim of the system," he explains. As a result, he found himself evaluating resources from the archives in terms of their validity and originality rather than by their objective truth. Each insight he gathered from his research, he explained, merely illustrated one aspect from among a "multitude of truths."

What lessons can we draw from this? First, that archival institutions have tremendous power:

- The power to decide which information is captured, and which is ignored (or "lost")

- The power to grant or deny access to the data, or to limit the time or type of interactions people and systems can have with it

- The power to classify and tag information in ways that shape how others think about, use, or interpret it

- The power to make finding information easy or difficult

- The power to effect political control over ideas, even long after the politics have faded

According to Tesar, you can't divorce the use of a data archive from the ethical implications of interacting with and interpreting the data it contains. Even for something as seemingly innocuous as time zone information, it's important to know *who created it, and why they created it, and what challenges they faced* in building the "source of truth" that you see before you.

Each of us can interpret data in any way we want, and because of that, we have an ethical obligation to be aware of our own personal lens and biases. Those who disagree with what you believe to be right might be objectively wrong, but are not inferior, bad or stupid. Instead, they have different experiences and are applying their own values to generate a different perspective than yours. Recognizing this can help you take the first step towards ethical interpretation.

The truth you might find in an archive of data can often be elusive, but sometimes just knowing what people *thought* was true at a particular time can be tremendously useful.

THE BOTTOM LINE

According to Deming, what is true is not necessarily useful, and besides – the pursuit of truth can be extensive and expensive. (Radziwill, 2019) Rather, it's *knowledge* and understanding we need to focus on pursuing. Your truth might be keeping your company small, or holding you hostage to limiting beliefs. Knowledge, in contrast, helps us understand how systems function so that we can anticipate what will happen next.

"Truth" originates from multiple sources, and is shaped by those who interpret it. It emerges over time (and sometimes not at all). One person or governing body's truth may or may not be another's, and many "sources of truth" are just made-up conventions that people have grown to accept because those standards ease communications. A person's response to what is presented as a truth, even for something as seemingly straightforward as time zones, can be innocuous, emotional, aggressive, or even violent. Controlling the narrative can bring power to one party over another, or obfuscate the actions of enemies and competitors.

When you interact with an archive of data (or any other critical information resource), you're engaging with its *entire political history*. This includes how the data was created, the backgrounds and biases of the people who originally created it, the people who currently act as its guardians, and the power those people or institutions have been formally or informally incentivized to uphold. When interacting with data or information resources, it is crucial to consider the entire political history and the networks of influence surrounding them.

The pursuit of truth can be costly and might not always be useful or beneficial. Truth is subjective, shaped by multiple sources and interpretations, and always influenced by political and social factors.

Once we understand how much imperfection our organization is willing to accept, based on our risk appetite, we can make better decisions about how much time and effort to invest in cleaning data and making meaning from it.

REFERENCES

Bell Labs. (1962). About Time. *Bell System Science Series.* Documentary (52 minutes). Available from https://www.youtube.com/watch?v=e__emnxC2Gc

Costa-Font, J., Fleche, S. & Pagan, R. (2021, July). The Welfare Effects of Time Reallocation: Evidence from Daylight Saving Time. CESifo Working Papers, ISSN 2364-1428 (electronic version). Munich Society for the Promotion of Economic Research, Ludwigs-Maximilians University's Center for Economic Studies and the IFO Institute. Available from https://www.econstor.eu/bitstream/10419/245376/1/cesifo1_wp9195.pdf

IndyStar. (2018, November 27). How Indiana went from 'God's time' to split zones and daylight-saving. *IndyStar.* Available from https://www.indystar.com/story/news/politics/2018/11/27/indianapolis-indiana-time-zone-history-central-eastern-daylight-savings-time/2126300002/.

Moser, W. (2012, March 12). Daylight Saving Time: Way More Complicated Than Just Setting Your Clocks Back. *Chicago Magazine.* Available from https://www.chicagomag.com/city-life/march-2012/daylight-savings-time-way-more-complicated-than-just-setting-your-clocks-back/

Murphy, K. (2019, June 21). What time is it? For ICANN, even that can be a controversial question. *Domain Incite.* Available from https://domainincite.com/24428-what-time-is-it-for-icann-even-that-can-be-a-controversial-question

Nosowitz, D. (2022, March 22). Daylight Saving Time Is Actually a Good Thing. *Popular Mechanics.* Available from https://www.popularmechanics.com/science/environment/a18011/in-defense-of-daylight-saving-time/

Radziwill, N. M. (2019, March 2). Imperfect action is better than perfect inaction: What Harry Truman can teach us about loss functions. *Quality & Innovation.* Available from https://qualityandinnovation.com/2019/03/02/imperfect-action-is-better-than-perfect-inaction-what-harry-truman-can-teach-us-about-loss-functions-with-an-intro-to-ggplot/

Rosehill, D. (2021, October 3). The Largely Untold Story of How One Guy In California Keeps The World's Computers Running On The Right Time Zone. (Well, Sort Of). *One Zero.* Available from https://onezero.medium.com/the-largely-untold-story-of-how-one-guy-in-california-keeps-the-worlds-computers-on-the-right-time-a97a5493bf73

Shammas, B. (2022, March 18). Why people hated permanent daylight saving time when the U.S. last tried it. *Washington Post.* Available from https://www.washingtonpost.com/history/2022/03/18/daylight-saving-seventies-history/

Tesar., M. (2015). Ethics and truth in archival research. *History of Education.* 44(1), pp. 101-114.

UCLA Samueli School of Engineering. (2022, March 10). "Time Zone King": How One UCLA Computer Scientist Keeps Digital Clocks Ticking. Available from https://samueli.ucla.edu/time-zone-king-how-one-ucla-computer-scientist-keeps-digital-clocks-ticking/

United States Department of Transportation (USDOT). (2022, September 20). DOT Can Improve Processes for Evaluating the Impact of Time Zone

Changes and Promoting Uniform Time Observance. Report ST2022037, Office of the Inspector General. Available from https://www.oig.dot.gov/sites/default/files/DOT%20Time%20Zone%20Final%20Report%209-20-22.pdf

Wade, G. (2021, November 5). How Daylight Saving Time Can Take a Toll on Your Mental Health—And What To Do To Boost Your Mood. *Health*. Available from https://www.health.com/mind-body/dst-mental-health

Wallace, G. (2022, September 22). DOT to map out nation's time zones after report shows no official map exists. *CNN Politics Blog*. Available from https://www.cnn.com/2022/09/22/politics/time-zone-map-transportation-department/index.html

CHAPTER 2

BEWARE OF YOUR OWN BRAIN

"The first principle is that you must not fool yourself - and you are the easiest person to fool. So you have to be very careful about that."
- Richard Feynman, physicist

Richard Stockton Rush III had always been an intelligent and fearless guy. A commercial pilot by the age of 19, he completed an undergraduate degree in aerospace engineering at Princeton, and later an MBA from Berkeley. After working as a test pilot, he quickly assumed various leadership positions at the intersection of business and science. Over time, his adventurous spirit became more enraptured by deep-sea exploration.

In 2009, he co-founded a company with a vision to develop, build, and lease fleets of underwater submersibles to make deep sea tourism a reality. By 2010, OceanGate Expeditions was already taking passengers, dubbed "mission specialists" in their contracts and liability waivers, in experimental submersibles built using a titanium hull.

The company quickly pivoted to a carbon fiber hull, a lightweight material that maintains buoyancy at the cost of added fragility. OceanGate hired the contractor that had designed (but never deployed) a composites-based vessel to explore the deepest part of the Pacific Ocean to achieve this feat, giving them a six-week timeline. The engineering community, recognizing this as bold and risky, were impressed that the contractor could even deliver in that short time span. (Sloan, 2017)

But by 2017, cracks were beginning to form, impacting the structural integrity of the company. OceanGate's Director of Marine Operations, David Lochridge, had expressed concerns about various aspects of the vessel's design, including a viewport that hadn't been certified for the target depth of the submersible and the integrity of the novel carbon fiber hull. He had raised many flags verbally, all the way up to CEO Rush, but felt like his concerns weren't being taken seriously. This was doubly concerning to Lochridge since his role was responsible for the safety of crew and staff on expeditions.

On January 18, 2018, Lochridge formally submitted his concerns in a report. (Court documents suggest that it was written at the request of the CEO.) On January 19, a company meeting was held to discuss the report. OceanGate asserted that "Lochridge repeatedly refused to accept the veracity of information provided by the company's lead engineer" and "would not authorize any manned tests" of the vessel. In short, Lochridge was impeding progress. The company terminated him on the spot.

But an event with curious timing happened less than two months later: CEO Rush received a letter signed by 38 industry experts. The letter warned of potentially catastrophic consequences and advised that the company invest in a stringent, data-driven quality assurance process. "We recommend that at a minimum you institute a prototype testing program that is reviewed and witnessed by [DNL, a quality assurance and risk management for the maritime industry]. While this may demand additional time and expense, it is our unanimous view that this validation process by a third-party is a critical component in the safeguards that protect all submersible occupants." (MTS, 2018) On March 22, industry expert Rob McCallum, Founder of EYOS Expeditions, emailed Rush. "As much as I appreciate entrepreneurship and innovation," he said, "you are potentially putting an entire industry at risk."

Rush was incensed. Four days later, he replied to McCallum. "I know that our engineering focused, innovative approach (as opposed to an existing standards compliance focused design process) flies in the face of the submersible orthodoxy, but that is the nature of innovation. I have grown tired of industry players who try to use a safety argument to stop innovation… We have heard the baseless cries of 'you are going to kill someone' way too often. I take this as a serious personal insult." (Morelle et al., 2023)

How could Rush's colleagues outside the company have known about these issues?

OceanGate had its suspicions. In June 2018, the company filed a lawsuit alleging that Lochridge had violated the terms of his nondisclosure, "to hold [the company's] confidential information in strict confidence, and not to disparage OceanGate or its business or products." (OceanGate v. Lochridge, 2018a) The court filing strongly suggests that Lochridge just used OceanGate for visa and residency purposes, and that Lochridge was reckless, sharing secrets as "casual small talk." But safety violations aren't protected as "secrets" in most courts of law.

While not an engineer, Lochridge was certified as a diver and undersea inspector, and was qualified to monitor and address issues related to safety, which were part of his job description. He felt that he was dismissed in retaliation for raising safety issues and filed a countersuit. In it, he called out three critical issues: the viewport, failures identified by testing the scale model of the submersible that remained unresolved, and the "the lack of non-destructive testing performed on the hull." (OceanGate v.

Lochridge, 2018b) While the carbon fiber was more naturally buoyant than its steel and titanium predecessors, it was also much more subject to sudden failure under compressive stress, the kind of stress that defines the hostile physics of the deep sea.

Rush was quick to reassure passengers, crew, and courts. The Titan submersible was equipped with a state-of-the-art acoustic monitoring and data management system, *so* innovative that Rush held the patent on it. (OceanGate, 2018) But, as expressed in Lochridge's response to Ocean Gate's initial filing, "this type of acoustic analysis would only show when a component is about to fail - often milliseconds before an implosion - and would not detect any existing flaws prior to putting pressure onto the hull." (OceanGate v. Lochridge, 2018b) No corrective action can be launched or completed on a timescale shorter than the human brain can register the signal.

A huge fan of *The Checklist Manifesto* which sat prominently on a table in the ship's lounge, Rush maintained a strong cultural focus on safety for everything *but* the design and testing of the submersible. All repairs were followed by a five-minute period of reflection where staff could double check their work. A "three strikes rule" was in place to cancel a dive where three issues were noted at once. The entire crew went through a long checklist each morning to assure mission readiness. (Weissman, 2023)

---

*"You know, at some point, **safety just is pure waste.** I mean, if you just want to be safe, don't get out of bed, don't get in your car, don't do anything. At some point you're gonna take some risk, and it really is a risk/reward question. I think I can do this just as safely by breaking the rules."*
- Doomed diver Stockton Rush to David Pogue (2022)

While OceanGate and Lochridge settled out of court, in November

2018, it is unclear whether safety issues associated with the design had been addressed to any extent. Plus, there had never been a fatal accident in the submersible community, so there was some resistance around the repeated warnings. The catastrophic implosion of the Titan submersible on June 18, 2023 that claimed five lives, including CEO Rush, suggests that the leader continued to stake his life (and the lives of his passengers) on the *belief* that acoustic monitoring would provide enough early warning for the vessel to resurface.

This belief would remain unchallenged by the company's engineers (who were subject to the power differential between the CEO and the team, possibly inhibiting them from voicing counterpoints) and unchallenged by the data that could have produced by non-destructive testing and served as the basis for external review. Not long after the disaster, a former accountant (who turned down the role of "chief pilot" after Lochridge was fired) revealed that most of the engineers were part-time or early career, suggesting that the power differential was even more significant. (Loh 2023) The combination of these effects created the conditions for impending disaster.

YOUR BIGGEST ENEMY

"It wouldn't be me," you might say. "If *I* were the OceanGate CEO, I'd *definitely* have demanded the data that would enable a qualified third party to certify the vessel."

But you might not. There's one unavoidable thing you and Stockton Rush have in common: you both have *human brains*. You're limited by them, and subject to the biochemistry and biases therein... in particular, the inability to accurately assess risk given your own confidence, convictions, and fears. And whether you saw the danger or not, your fear might cause you to be unduly influenced by the power dynamics around you. It's hard to confront someone with more power than you, even when you're moved by a strong conviction (like saving lives). The human brain's survival instincts kick in, preserving its own relationships and financial well-being.

---

*"Data can provide insight or be used to mislead. When looking at data, you need to **critically think about how you could be misled**."*
- John Hunter, CEO of Curious Cat Management

Regarding data-driven decision making, *your brain* is your biggest enemy. Humans tend to seek out and interpret information that confirms our existing beliefs or hypotheses, while disregarding or downplaying contradictory evidence. This confirmation bias can lead to decisions based on incomplete or biased information, limiting our ability to objectively evaluate risks. Recency bias can lead you to overemphasize recent or more vivid events, skewing your perception of risk. Additionally, brains are susceptible to framing effects, where the way information is presented influences how we make decisions. As a result, we might make different choices based on how data is presented to us, rather than the reality indicated by the data itself.

To complicate matters, even one catastrophic loss is unlikely to motivate someone to think differently the next time a similar scenario is presented. While it's comparatively easy for people to learn, it is remarkably difficult for them to *unlearn* incorrect or outdated information, even when it's necessary. (de Holan et al., 2004) This is why we need each other's perspectives and interpretations of data. This is also why we need to remain conscious of the power dynamics that can lead to manipulation or suppression of data-driven insights.

RISK APPETITE AND ACCOUNTABILITY

The same data, however, can be interpreted in completely different ways based on the risk appetite of the person evaluating the data. That is, what if you (or your organization's) willingness and capacity to accept and tolerate risks while in pursuit of your goals and objectives?

People and organizations with a low risk appetite tend to be cautious and conservative. In the context of data management, they may implement stringent security measures, restrict access to sensitive information, and maintain strict compliance with regulations for protecting personally identifiable information (PII).

---

*"I just couldn't get comfortable ultimately with the design of Titan because **there was so little data available** about managing that risk and really what it looked like if this sub went up and down as many times as it was going to."*

- Josh Gates, who chose not to take his film crew on the Titan submersible

---

People and organizations with a moderate risk appetite strike a balance between caution and innovation. They may invest in predictive analytics, conduct periodic risk assessments, and establish thresholds for acceptable levels of failures.

In contrast, organizations with a high risk appetite take calculated risks, usually ensuring they have the necessary safeguards and contingency plans in place to mitigate negative outcomes. Your penchant for risk will color your dominant narrative and become the lens through which you evaluate opportunity and reward.

> *"[Stockton Rush] had so much passion for the project that he **was blinded by it**. He wasn't objective and he didn't look at things that I saw and that others saw that were problematic... because **they didn't fit his narrative.**"*
> *- Jay Bloom, investor who turned down a spot on the doomed Titan submersible*

Decisions made based on data are also impacted by *who* has been designated as accountable for those decisions. When an *accountable* person has more decision authority than a person *impacted* by a decision, they can make decisions that reduce potential consequences for them personally while increasing the likelihood of negative consequences for those affected. It is human nature to seek out our own survival, even when we survive at the expense of others.

DEADLY DECISIONS

Rushing the introduction of a product, adopting cost-cutting measures that compromise quality or neglecting crucial testing of design elements, can create a hazardous environment where people face a heightened risk of injury or death. When these dangerous decisions are made, the data that could have led to a different outcome is *often* available but ignored or suppressed by people in power.

And it doesn't take *much* power to ensure that a deadly decision is made. On one Monday morning in January, director Allan McDonald had a tough decision to make: sign off on a rocket launch the next day or withhold approval. According to the data he had received, a critical component of the vehicle wasn't rated for performance in cold weather, and there was an increased chance that it could fail, compromising the mission. While they were confident that the component would function properly above 53 degrees Fahrenheit, the temperatures the next morning were projected to be in the upper teens. He didn't have any data that conclusively indicated the component would fail at low temperatures, but he also didn't have data that suggested otherwise. He withheld his signature.

But his attempt was futile... those in power above him quickly overruled his position and made their displeasure clear. There was pressure from people in power all the way up the chain. Executives and mid-level managers at Morton Thiokol, the contractor responsible for the component, feared that its vendor status would be removed if the launch was delayed, potentially threatening other business that the company was hoping to secure with NASA. The White House had promised the nation the "first teacher in space" and the State of the Union address where it would be celebrated was approaching. Every day with a delay meant a delay for the whole launch schedule. And NASA felt increased pressure to launch in light of a continuous stream of nightly news, highlighting delays and suggesting a lack of competence. "Pictures of frustrated technicians in white suits accompanied a narrative of failure: a screw that was stuck, batteries that were too weak to operate a drill, a drill bit that crumbled, and finally, the use of a hacksaw. The piece conveyed the impression that NASA technicians, though prudent and cautious, were bumblers." (Ignatius, 1986)

After the Challenger explosion on January 28, 1986 that claimed the lives of all seven astronauts on board, McDonald would be called to testify in the Presidential Commission. As a result of his candor, he was demoted from his position and marginalized by his peers as a whistleblower. By the time the investigation was completed, McDonald was vindicated. Morton Thiokol elevated him to a vice president role, where he was able to address the root causes of the issues on which he staked his reputation.

NORMALIZATION OF DEVIANCE

While the Challenger case illustrates how competing interests and power dynamics can contribute to deadly decisions, nearly all players in the drama were intensely invested in the issue of whether or not to launch. Engineers who opposed the launch had data to drive their arguments, and executives who were in favor of the launch also had data and explanations to support their position. But similar dangers can arise from apathy or lack of engagement,

This apathy often results from a "box checking" culture, where work is completed to the "barest minimal standard." (Raso, 2016) This normalizes *what* is done over *how or why* something is done, and establishes a tolerance for incremental deviations that can increase over time. In politics, this is called the Overton Window, reflecting the shifting extreme behaviors and political outcomes that people come to find as "normal." (Russell, 2006) It shouldn't be surprising that the "normalization of deviance" effect was identified as a result of studying the Challenger disaster. (Vaughan 1996)

When deviations go uncorrected, some people begin to believe that there's no reason to worry about them, and start to tolerate wider deviations. *People responsible for the deviations keep deviating.* One of the most egregious examples of this is the story of B-52 pilot Bud Holland, and the "failed leadership and command climate which had degenerated into an unhealthy state of apathy and non-compliance" that ended with the fiery deaths of all four aboard his aircraft on June 24, 1994. (Kern 1995)

Bud was a man of myth and legend. While some praised him as the "best B-52 pilot ever," others referred to him as a rogue, and multiple colleagues refused to fly with him, fearing for their own lives. He flew too low, too fast, and took turns too steeply. He had taken a class early in his career where the instructor explained maneuvers that should only be used in life-or-death war situations; Bud, it is said, claimed that he wouldn't have been shown these possibilities if the aircraft couldn't handle them. Throughout his career, he dangerously pushed the limits of the aircraft, and his superiors neglected to send a clear message that this was unacceptable. "Supervision and leadership facilitated the accident through failed policies of selective enforcement of regulations, as well as failing to heed to desperate warning signals raised by peers and subordinates over a period of three years prior to the accident." (Kern 1995) Whether data is formally collected or not, oftentimes, *people are aware of issues.*

What does Bud's case tell us about data? First, collecting and tracking data can help keep you honest about when and where deviations occur. Selective enforcement is much more difficult when reliable data is available and visible. Second, recorded data can help to compel the actions that pull people back into compliance. To be data-driven means to take appropriate action based on the evidence presented in each situation.

THE BOTTOM LINE

Confidence, conviction, apathy, fear, and ignorance are the cardinal sins that can turn your brain against you when data-driven decision making is needed. You can mitigate the risks of these factors by promoting transparency, by making decisions as teams, by confronting the power dynamics around decision making, and by calling attention to different risk appetites. When we work to gain consensus with other data-driven people who also value evidence, it will help keep us honest with ourselves, and manage the inner demons catalyzed by our default brain chemistry.

"We all have blind spots and we all fall prey to the operational glitches of our brains. No one is immune. Checking ourselves isn't nearly enough… actively seek out other views and perspectives [and acknowledge] blind spots…

Perhaps most of all, we need to have a sense of humility. It's far too easy to be impressed with ourselves and far too difficult to see how we're being led astray. There is often a negative correlation between our level of certainty and the likelihood of us being wrong. We all need to make an effort to believe less of what we think."
- Greg Satell, global change and transformation expert, on LinkedIn (June 24, 2023)

If you're a manager or executive, failure to heed the data-driven warnings of the engineers and specialists you employ may ultimately be your undoing. But in so many cases, there will be no consequences (at least not before you're on to your next job). As a result, you'll make bad decisions repeatedly, and because no one ends up dead on your watch, you'll continue ignoring data and the people who bring you insights and warnings based on it.

"People fear what they don't understand. And people hate what they fear. As an executive storyteller, if you want to protect against hate and fear, be patient and always be willing to explain."
– T. Scott Clendaniel, VP of AI at Analytics Edge

We praise the ethics and courage of people like McDonald years after cover-ups become known, while continuing to create the conditions for human nature to win, every time, over data. Every disaster movie, after all, starts with decision makers ignoring the advice of a data-driven scientist.

REFERENCES

de Holan, P. M., Phillips, N., & Lawrence, T. B. (2004). Managing organizational forgetting. MIT Sloan Management Review. Available from https://sloanreview.mit.edu/article/managing-organizational-forgetting/

Dowd, K. (2023, June 21). Missing Titanic submersible CEO Stockton Rush is from prominent San Francisco family. SFGate. Available from https://www.sfgate.com/bayarea/article/missing-titanic-submersible-ceo-sf-family-18162447.php

Ignatius, D. (1986, March 30). Did the Media Goad NASA Into the Challenger Disaster? *Washington Post*. Available from https://www.washingtonpost.com/archive/opinions/1986/03/30/did-the-media-goad-nasa-into-the-challenger-disaster/e0c8669d-a809-4c8d-a4f8-50652b892274/

Kern, T. (1995). Darker shades of blue: A case study of failed leadership. L200, Developing Leaders and Organizations, by CGSC/Department of Command and Leadership, 321-342. Available from https://convergentperformance.com/wp-content/uploads/attachments/Darker_Shades_of_Blue.pdf

Loh, M. (2023, July 3). OceanGate's former finance director said she quit when Stockton Rush asked her to be the Titanic submersible's chief pilot after firing the original one for raising safety issues: report. Yahoo! News. Available from https://www.yahoo.com/news/oceangates-former-finance-director-said-051737973.html

Marine Technology Society (MTS). (2018, March 27). Letter to OceanGate CEO signed by 38 industry experts. Available from https://int.nyt.com/data/documenttools/marine-technology-society-committee-2018-letter-to-ocean-gate/eddb63615a7b3764/full.pdf

Morelle, R., Francis, A. & Evans, G. (2023, June 23). Titan sub CEO dismissed safety warnings as 'baseless cries', emails show. BBC News. Available from https://www.bbc.com/news/world-us-canada-

65998914

OceanGate (2018, March 8). Systems and methods for curing, testing, validating, rating, and monitoring the integrity of composite structures. Patent #11119071. Available from
https://patents.justia.com/patent/11119071

OceanGate vs. Lochridge. (2018a, June 25). Available from
https://storage.courtlistener.com/recap/gov.uscourts.wawd.262471/gov
.uscourts.wawd.262471.1.1.pdf

OceanGate vs. Lochridge. (2018b, August 15). Available from
https://storage.courtlistener.com/recap/gov.uscourts.wawd.262471/gov
.uscourts.wawd.262471.7.0.pdf

Pogue, D. (2023, June 25). OceanGate CEO's 2022 interviews on Titan sub's design, safety. Yahoo! News. Available from
https://news.yahoo.com/oceangate-ceos-2022-interviews-titan-143117356.html

Raso, R. (2016). Checking the box. *Nursing Management.* doi:
10.1097/01.NUMA.0000502805.22177.1f

Russell, N. J. (2006). An introduction to the Overton window of political possibilities. Mackinac Center for Public Policy, 4. Available from
https://www.mackinac.org/7504

Sloan, J. (2017, May 10). Composite submersibles: Under pressure in deep, deep waters. *CompositesWorld.* Available from
https://www.compositesworld.com/articles/composite-submersibles-under-pressure-in-deep-deep-waters

Vaughan D. (1996). The Challenger Launch Decision. Risky Technology, Culture, and Deviance at NASA. Chicago, IL: University of Chicago Press.

Weissman, A. (2023, June 21). Mission Titanic, Part 2: Delays and an unsettling statement from the OceanGate CEO. *Travel Weekly.* Available from https://www.travelweekly.com/North-America-Travel/Mission-Titanic-Part-2

CHAPTER 3

BEWARE OF OTHER PEOPLE

"No one joins a cult."
-- Mark Vicente, Writer/Director/Producer in The Vow

While data, analytics, and artificial intelligence (AI) can be used to inform, empower, and liberate good ideas from the irrationality of power games... they can also just as easily *become* tools of abuse, coercion, and control. It's impossible to successfully manage data and AI without considering the power dynamics of the environment that *produced* it – and will *use* it.

At Taiwan Semiconductor Manufacturing Company (TSMC), for example, excitement ran high in 2020. The company had started construction on their new Arizona facility, catalyzed by billions of dollars of U.S. grants and loans. The mission was larger than life: to improve the health of supply chains by enabling customers to provide their own specifications and have chips built to specification. American workers are required to spend up to a year at the company's facilities in Taiwan, experiencing immersion in the company's culture and shadowing more senior Taiwanese employees.

Since its genesis in 1987, TSMC has gained near mythical status in Taiwan. Some citizens refer to it as "the divine mountain that guards the nation" because of its geopolitical value, an asset that many countries might protect to maintain the processors that drive their economies. The sense of loyalty and admiration to the company is palpable in that country. But inside the company's Arizona operations, the vibe was not as buoyant. Early in 2024, Violet Zhou at *Rest of World* magazine interviewed nearly 20 current and former TSMC employees. Their identities were kept anonymous because many feared retaliation from the company.

American TSMC employees described the work environment as rigorous, exacting, and demanding. Employees were routinely expected to come in early, put in long days, take overnight calls, and provide support on weekends or holidays. During onsite training months in Taiwan, most meetings and updates were held in Mandarin, and many American employees found Google Translate to be only minimally helpful. American employees felt that the language barrier was even being held against them: they were still impossibly accountable for all the information in meetings, briefings, and documents.

Even when employees were unable to participate fully, they were held accountable. Public shaming and humiliation was commonplace, and employees were regularly threatened with termination. When Americans brought these concerns to HR, managers were instructed to be less volatile, but the behavior did not relent. Managers would frequently conduct "stress tests" – urgent, substantial assignments to be completed before the end of the day or week – to gauge the Americans employees' dedication, commitment, and willingness to sacrifice for the company. One former employee reported the "false sense of urgency with every... task, [pushing you] to finish everything immediately... [which is] just not realistic for people that want to have some normal work-life balance." Urgency was being used as a means of control and oppression, and a punitive mindset meant that criticism was valued more than encouragement. Not everyone works well this way.

THE DATA SUFFERS

When a work environment is characterized by unreasonable demands, unquestioning loyalty, or the continual fear of punishment, *data and data operations suffer*. It's not as easy to get the time required to produce solid, rigorous data and maintain the robust pipelines and provenance that requires. It's more difficult to act with courage, presenting data and analytics that are robustly produced, rather than producing the information that leaders demand to see.

In situations like this, when the survival of one's job is at stake, human nature takes over. Employees will optimize for speed over data integrity if that's what they're being rewarded for doing. They will be more willing to manipulate outcomes to avoid public or private shaming. After all, just matching a leader's expectation of what data should show is *far less painful* than taking a stand for accuracy and integrity.

---

*"Five former employees from the U.S. told Rest of World that TSMC engineers sometimes falsified or cherry-picked data for customers and managers. Sometimes, the engineers said, **staff would manipulate data from testing tools or wafers to please managers who had seemingly impossible expectations**.*

*Other times, one engineer said, 'because the workers were spread so thin, **anything they could do to get work off their plate they would do**.' Four American employees described TSMC culture as 'save face': Workers would strive to make a team, a department, or the company look good at the expense of efficiency and employee wellbeing."*
(Zhou, 2024)

This phenomenon is not limited to companies like TSMC that operate across distinctly different Asian and American work cultures. In 2015, auto manufacturer Volkswagen was called to account in U.S. Congressional hearings for falsifying emissions data using onboard "defeat devices." (O'Kane, 2015) Engineers tampered with the emissions reporting because they knew there would be personal and professional consequences (ie. that they might lose their jobs) if they didn't deliver on acceleration requirements, fuel economy, and emissions.

Data integrity suffers when people can be punished for what it reveals. Survival wins every time.

TOXICITY IS RELATIVE

But these dynamics aren't always perceived as bad by the people in the affected workplaces. While the work environment was described as "toxic" by most Americans at TSMC, *very few* of the Taiwanese provided the same opinion. Taiwanese employees were accustomed to spending tens of hours on status reports, and didn't see that time as an infringement on their other work time or their personal lives.

They believed that it was *disrespectful* to challenge their superiors, and that following orders was the *only* acceptable option. Independent thought was not something this group expected or valued. In the words of one Taiwanese worker at the Phoenix plant, "everything comes from working hard. Without this culture, TSMC cannot be number one in the world... *it's my religion.*"

THE DARK SIDE OF DEDICATION

When you believe in a mission or a cause strongly enough, it can hold an esteemed position in your life. Many people are deeply dedicated to their church, their religion or denomination, their political party, or their family. Some of us are dedicated to a company that - with an investment of their own sweat equity - will accomplish great things and make the world a better place.

Such was the case with the small but enterprising professional development organization, founded in 1998, that had a commendable mission: to help people *experience more joy* in their lives. Who doesn't want more joy? The company had not only a proven series of programs, but a committed community of satisfied customers. In fact, every person promoting their offerings had been a customer, and had *themselves* experienced the resurgence of joy that the workshops promised.

Despite its early success, NXIVM would *not* go down in history as an organization that empowered millions through self-help. Rather, NXIVM will be remembered as a pyramid scheme and sex cult. Its leader, Keith Raniere, was convicted of racketeering, sex trafficking, and exploiting members through forced labor, exposing the sinister underbelly of the group's manipulative and criminal practices through detailed testimonies in court proceedings. The NXIVM scandal demonstrated how even legitimate organizations can devolve culturally into coercive, abusive cults under charismatic leadership.

Mark Vicente, a filmmaker deeply involved in NXIVM for 12 years before ultimately testifying against Raniere in court, explains how easy it is for well-meaning participants to get caught up in cult behavior. First, he cites social worker Amy Morin, who defines a cult as "an organized group whose purpose is to dominate cult members through psychological manipulation and pressure strategies... usually headed by a powerful leader who isolates members from the rest of society."

He reminds us that *people inside the cult can't see that they are* inside a cult: "They are in the equivalent of an authoritarian regime and they have completely bought into the ideology. Do not give them ammunition to believe you are the enemy by attacking them. Stay interested in their perspective, and above all, be loving and kind. One day they might compare what they are TOLD is love (in the cult) to the ACTUAL love you are giving them and realize they prefer your unconditional kindness to the fear and punishment they are experiencing." (Vicente, 2023)

Everyone has wounds, and many people (actively or passively) seek ways to heal them. The promise of healing and belonging, and the *relief* from deep, existential pain this can provide, is often enough for people to miss seeing the damage that is being done to them. The extreme empathy that is often expressed by colleagues in these environments is, more likely than not, being offered with a purpose in mind.

---

*"**Empathy is not absolution**. You can internalize the ideas of others and still vehemently disagree. There is a reason that Special Forces are trained to understand the cultures in which they will operate and it isn't because it makes them nicer people. **It's because it makes them more lethal operators.**"*

-- Greg Satell, in https://digitaltonto.com/2023/how-empathy-can-be-your-secret-weapon/

TRAITS OF HIGH-DEMAND GROUPS

One of the common characteristics of cults, according to Vicente, is that they place high *demands* on their members - in terms of participation, loyalty, and prioritization. Activities required by the group *must* take precedence over other aspects of the participant's life, or their loyalty and dedication may be subtly questioned. Even the International Cultic Studies Assc (ICSA) calls cults *high-demand groups.*

Burkley (2020) uses the NXIVM case to identify three general characteristics of cult environments that, they explain, can sneak up on (and gradually ensnare) even healthy individuals:

- **Obedience**: The group is commanded by a single leader (or a small, tight-knit group of leaders). The supreme authority of the leader is never questioned, and individuals may be "tested" to ensure willingness to quickly take on anything the leader requests. Questioning the leader may be considered disobedience or lack of trust, and those who refuse to be "accountable" are shamed, punished, or isolated.

- **Deindividuation**: Individuals are reminded that they are only there to do a job, and they are replaceable. Sometimes they are reminded that there are many other people who would do anything to take their place. Gradually, people are disengaged from their identity and agency, and become more compliant.

- **Depletion**: Unreasonable demands, excessive workloads, and flimsy boundaries are used to reduce self-control and willpower. When people cannot meet these demands, they are held up against real or imagined people who *could*, thus advancing deindividuation. The less physical, mental, and emotional energy someone has, the more they will tend towards unquestioned obedience.

Those same characteristics sometimes emerge in businesses with a charismatic leader at the helm (or even academic departments with authoritarian deans). You *must* obey authority without question; you have *no* livelihood without the organization (and they can replace you easily, so don't get too comfortable); and they will work you to the bone (because not only do you owe them, you *want* to work hard because you feel lucky to be a part of this exclusive group).

Notice how closely these characteristics track with *expected, honorable behaviors* in a company. Conforming to the direction identified by leadership is necessary, as is balancing individual identity with group identity to form solid collaborative teams; and of course you may have to go above and beyond the call of duty to meet the needs of the business, at times. In cultic organizations, positive behaviors are corrupted... slowly, gently, subtly... until the leader is assured of the deference he or she demands.

CONSEQUENCES FOR DATA INTEGRITY & AI

While the analogy of cult dynamics may seem extreme, exploring edge cases can help us understand how and whether unhealthy situations can emerge. Both *culture* and *cult* share the Latin root *cultus*, which means to inhabit, grow, or worship. In a work environment, we come together with others, inhabiting the mission of the organization to grow its impact and potential. We can *choose* who or what to worship, though, and whether our commitment will even run that deep.

Debilitating work routines and pressure or shaming to conform, as shadow elements of a workplace culture, can significantly compromise data integrity in several ways:

- **Burnout and exhaustion**: Employees subjected to grueling work schedules and unrealistic expectations are more likely to make careless mistakes when entering, processing, or analyzing data due to fatigue and lack of focus.

- **Fear and intimidation**: A culture of public shaming and humiliation creates an environment of fear, where employees may be tempted to manipulate or falsify data to avoid scrutiny or criticism, even unintentionally.

- **Lack of transparency**: Toxic cultures breed secrecy and lack of open communication. Employees may hesitate to report data errors or inconsistencies out of fear of repercussions, allowing data integrity issues to persist.

- **High turnover**: Oppressive work environments lead to high employee turnover, resulting in loss of institutional knowledge and consistent data management practices, increasing the risk of data integrity breaches.

- **Ethical compromises**: When employees are demoralized and dehumanized, they may become more susceptible to rationalizing unethical behavior, such as data falsification or manipulation, to cope or retaliate against the toxic environment.

The damage doesn't stop with mental health and well-being. Organizations where people express high levels of depletion are also associated with more, and more severe, cybersecurity incidents. (Nobles 2022; Hong et al., 2023) A summary of how ISA's cult characteristics might influence the behavior of data teams is presented in Table 1. Maintaining data integrity requires a culture of trust, transparency, and psychological safety, where employees feel empowered to report issues without fear of retribution and are provided with appropriate resources and support to ensure data accuracy and quality.

Cult Characteristic (from ISCA, 1996)	Impact on Data/AI Production & Use
A living leader whose members display zealous, unquestioning commitment	Analysts might provide the leader with data they want or expect to see, sacrificing data integrity
Focus on bringing in new members/hiring	There will always be the potential for new people who are willing to compromise data integrity to be seen as a valuable new employee
A money-making imperative	Tactical, urgent requests may always take priority over foundational work
Questioning, doubt, and dissent are discouraged or even punished	Analysts may be less likely to push back when data is unavailable/ unclean, or analytics are unsound
Techniques are used to suppress doubts about the group and its leader(s), e.g. debilitating work routines, public shaming	Data teams are more likely to make careless mistakes due to fatigue and lack of focus.
Members must get permission from leaders for all hiring, budgeting, or planning decisions (no healthy delegation)	Needing to get permission can discourage risk-taking and hinder innovative exploration, ultimately hindering progress
The group is elitist, claiming a special, exalted status for itself, its leader(s), and members, e.g. hard to get into, hard to remain a member of, lofty mission where leader brings unparalleled expertise	Data professionals unconsciously self-censor or succumb to confirmation bias, overlooking or downplaying data that contradicts the desired narrative to avoid feeling guilty or being shunned by the team
The group has an us-vs-them mentality, for example creating sharp delineations between people who are culture fits vs people who are not	Analysts or business unit leaders may feel pressure to conform and fulfill requests that compromise their professional integrity
The group's leader is not accountable to any authorities	Without external oversight or governance, a leader has unchecked

	power, increasing the risk of data manipulation, misuse of AI systems, and prioritizing personal interests over pro-social ethical considerations and data integrity.
The group teaches or implies that its supposedly exalted ends justify means that members would have considered unethical before joining the group	Guilt-tripping can gradually erode ethical boundaries and desensitize data teams to compromising on principles of data integrity and objectivity, rationalizing unethical practices as necessary for the "greater good" of the organization.
The leadership induces guilt feelings in members to control them, e.g. reminding them how important a task or project is, or how important it is to do what's needed for the business	Professionals may hesitate to raise red flags or report data quality issues out of fear of being guilt-tripped or facing consequences for disagreeing
Members' subservience to the group (or its extreme demands on their time or priorities) causes them to cut ties with family and friends, and/or give up personal goals/activities that were of interest before joining the group	Analysts or business unit leaders may rely less on their own professional integrity and more on the judgments of the group, whether or not those judgments are ethical.
Members are encouraged to live and/or socialize with other group members	When external views or counterfactuals are not incorporated into decision making, the quality of decisions will be eroded.
Members are expected to devote inordinate amounts of time to the group	Working under psychological pressure and manipulation leads to low morale, burnout, and high turnover among data professionals and business unit leaders. Brain drain can result in a loss of institutional knowledge and experience, further jeopardizing data integrity.

Table 1. How cult characteristics can impact the integrity of data, analytics, and ultimately AI.

THE BOTTOM LINE

Psychological pressure to deliver desired results can be insidious. When guilt is used to manipulate, data professionals may feel pressured to produce findings or analyses that align with leadership's expectations, even if it means compromising data integrity or employing questionable methods. Since power dynamics have the potential to emerge between *any* pair of people, data massaging, cherry-picking, or outright falsification (motivated when survival needs take precedence over integrity) are likely to be present in *every* organization to some extent.

"Crocodiles are easy. They try to kill and eat you.
People are harder.
Sometimes they pretend to be your friend first."
- Steve Irwin in The Crocodile Hunter

But toxicity is relative, and what is toxic to one person (or culture) may be perfectly acceptable to another. This is the gray area where conflict can arise, and where expectations can be subtly and brilliantly violated.

To maintain the integrity of data and AI systems, it is crucial to have robust accountability measures in place, including independent oversight bodies, external audits, and clear paths for whistleblowing and reporting concerns. Accountability helps ensure adherence to ethical standards, data quality protocols, and responsible AI practices, fostering trust and transparency in the organization's use of data and AI technologies.

Most critically, accountability requires the uncomfortable work of diving into the shadows, calling out and confronting the power dynamics that can poison data, analytics, and AI. The business processes around producing and using data, and the AI-generated results that depend on it, *cannot be separated* from the cultural context within which that data is produced.

Healthy dedication to a company's mission and leadership is essential. But while data can be used to empower and liberate, it can also be used as a weapon for people to gain status, recognition, or domination over others. In these cases, it becomes the poison that slowly, gradually, and stealthily compromises the integrity of (otherwise functional) work environments.

REFERENCES

Burkley, M. (2020, November 18). "3 Psychological Principles Nxivm Used to Brainwash Its Members." *Psychology Today*. Available from https://www.psychologytoday.com/us/blog/the-social-thinker/202011/3-psychological-principles-nxivm-used-brainwash-its-members

Hong, Y., Kim, M. J., & Roh, T. (2023). Mitigating the Impact of Work Overload on Cybersecurity Behavior: The Moderating Influence of Corporate Ethics—A Mediated Moderation Analysis. Sustainability, 15(19), 14327.

International Cultic Studies Association (ICSA). (1996). Are You, or Is Someone You Know, Involved in a High-Demand Group or Movement ("cult")? Available from http://www.dreichel.com/Checklist_of_Cult_Characte.htm

Nobles, C. (2022). Stress, burnout, and security fatigue in cybersecurity: A human factors problem. HOLISTICA – Journal of Business and Public Administration, 13(1), 49-72.

O'Kane, S. (2015, October 8). Volkswagen America's CEO blames software engineers for emissions cheating scandal. *The Verge*. Available from https://www.theverge.com/2015/10/8/9481651/volkswagen-congressional-hearing-diesel-scandal-fault

Vicente, M. (2023, May 17). What is a Cult?
https://www.markvicente.com/thoughts/2023/5/15/what-is-a-cult

Zhou, V. (2024, April 23). "TSMC's debacle in the American desert." *Rest of World.* Available from https://restofworld.org/2024/tsmc-arizona-expansion/

CHAPTER 4

BEWARE OF COLLECTIVE DELUSION

"As one very senior manager [of the Piper Alpha Rig during the July 6, 1988 disaster] said to the Enquiry, 'I knew everything was alright because I got no reports of anything being wrong.'"
-- Sir Brian Appleton, Technical Assessor for the Cullen Enquiry

In the oil and gas industry, "condensate" is a low-density mixture of hydrocarbons that has the potential to ignite when mixed with air. Work on tanks, lines, or pumps that move condensate through a refinery must be closely controlled, including the information exchange between everyone who works on the component and everyone who is impacted by that work. Anyone who comes in contact with the subsystem needs to have an accurate, complete, and timely picture of the work status, or deadly decisions can inadvertently be made.

In industrial facilities, a "Permit to Work" (PTW) process is typically in place to manage the quality and the flow of information around potentially consequential maintenance activities. PTW ensures that risk assessment and mitigations are addressed before maintenance can be performed in hazardous environments, including training and preparing the people who will be doing the work. Permits can be issued for hot work, which involves "spark-producing operations" like welding, cutting, or brazing, and cold work, which does not have the potential to produce sparks. Lockout and tagout (LOTO) procedures are often followed, disabling equipment in advance to prevent unintended starts or discharges of energy.

On July 6, 1988, on the Piper Alpha platform in the North Sea, condensate pump A was taken out of service for regular preventive maintenance, with a permit to work issued to electrically isolate the component. Separately, the pressure relief valve downstream of pump A was also taken out of service for recertification. At 2pm, scaffolding was set up to give contractors access to the valve, and by 6pm, the valve had been removed and recertified. There wasn't enough time to reinstall it, though, without a lengthy process of requesting approval for overtime pay. The supervisor on duty, who was new to his job, didn't know how to process a permit to work that was incomplete, so he marked the device as "suspended" on the printed permit and dropped off the paperwork in the control room, leaving "blind flanges" as a stopgap where the pressure relief valve had been installed. (Shallcross 2013)

The new shift workers took over shortly after 6pm, and reviewed the status of the permit to work on pump A. They had no information about the status of pump B (presumably, the notes were still sitting on a desk in the control room) and the scaffolding had dutifully been removed, eliminating all clues to the present scenario.

At 9:50pm, pump B experienced a fault and couldn't be restarted. The operations team only had half an hour to prevent a costly production shutdown, so they decided to remove the permit to work from pump A and restore it so that production could continue. After all, preventive maintenance could wait just a little longer... there was no immediate danger.

They were unaware, however, that the nearby pressure valve was inoperable, because the information was not available to them.

This hazard became all too apparent a few minutes later, when an explosion ripped through the platform, rattling cups and dishes, shaking people out of their beds, and cutting off the main lighting.

A chain of cascading failures was unleashed, including the failure of the fire water deluge system (which was set to manual to protect the occasional diver who might pass by an intake pipe), the lack of backup communications after the personnel staffing the radio tower had to flee due to fire, and the uncertainty people experienced in the absence of disaster preparedness training and drills, and the conflicting directives issued from management during the panic. The fires would continue to burn for three weeks, incurring a total of $3.4B in damages in addition to the extensive loss of life.

A FALSE COMFORT

While only 2 people died in the initial explosion, 165 more died from smoke inhalation, many in the residence area of the platform. 61 people survived by breaking protocol, jumping off the platform into the sea and taking their chances in the cold, shark-filled waters, hopeful that a nearby support vessel would find them.

It wasn't easy to identify this chain of events that led to the disaster because it had to be forensically reconstructed over months, using interviews from survivors, video data, and reports from emergency response workers. This case was particularly challenging because "little physical evidence remained, and no senior member of Piper Alpha's management team survived." (MacLeod & Richardson 2018)

According to Steve Rae, who survived the blast and its aftermath,

"These points all suggest a lack of situational awareness and cognitive competence – demonstrated by a failure to respond to the signals and signs that were present, in advance, and during the escalation of events." (Rae 2018)

What helps us detect and respond to the signals and signs around us? Data. When we are data-driven, we use these signals to build shared understanding and compel coordinated action. While many organizations struggle with collecting and sharing accurate, complete, useful information, many more struggle to interpret those signs and signals in meaningful ways, preventing problems before they can occur. Particularly in safety management, Rae suggests that organizations compensate for this struggle by establishing rigorous safety procedures rather than instilling the behavioral or cognitive competencies of mastering those procedures.

THE SEVEN DELUSIONS

Better processes, better data, and more predictive analytics could certainly help people build behavioral and cognitive competencies. But safety experts like Corrie Pitzer point out that there can be stark unintended consequences from taking this perfectly logical approach, because those who *feel* safe tend to be less mindful and vigilant.

Elaborate systems of safety procedures, libraries of completed checklists, and endless training gives workers a false sense of comfort and causes them to miss the signals that could indicate impending danger. Pitzer (2016) examines seven delusions in safety management that reveal insights about how (and how not!) to manage data and analytics in an enterprise.

> *"It is not what we don't do, or do wrong, that causes modern disasters… it is what we do. **The same things in the culture that make us successful may also cause the disasters**. We slowly, incrementally, and insidiously float into disaster."* - Corrie Pitzer, Safety Expert

#1: The Delusion of Linear Causation. This refers to the erroneous belief that risk factors and events align in a simple, deterministic sequence that results in a specific outcome. This concept stems from the use of oversimplified models that assume incidents occur due to a linear progression of failures in defenses. This understanding is damaging because it perpetuates the illusion that reinforcing defenses (or adding tests) will be sufficient to prevent failures. This delusion can limit insights that can be gained from data, by ignoring the complex and often unpredictable interactions and influences that aren't part of those simple causal chains. **The remedy is to recognize the multiplicity inherent in complex systems:** there are always paths that are invisible and cannot be measured or modeled.

#2: The Delusion of Compliance. This is the false belief that strict adherence to procedures and regulations inherently ensures quality, safety, or any other characteristic they are in place to promote. Reason (2016) illustrated this paradox with examples where following safety protocols paradoxically led to fatalities. The delusion of compliance can lead individuals and organizations to become less responsive to emerging risks or threats, the result of overreliance on (and unquestioning trust in) established procedures. The belief that the work system is infallible may prevent people from deviating from prescribed procedures even when the data suggests otherwise. **The remedy is mindfulness**. A data-driven culture values critical thinking and responsiveness to unique situations and changing conditions. Rigid reliance on data standards or governance practices without considering the evolving context can lead people to overlook crucial risk factors or ignore the shifting external environment. This leaves the organization vulnerable to data downtime, breaches, or losses.

#3: The Delusion of Consistency. This is the mistaken belief that uniformity and standardization in management practices will always lead to better control of risks and hazards, protecting against failures. It manifests in the premise that workplaces should limit all variability and instill consistency through strict adherence to a multitude of rules, controls, and regulations. The underlying assumption is that consistency always enhances predictability by harmonizing work practices, thereby reducing risks. However, in complex and high-risk systems, risks are not static but constantly evolve. The delusion of consistency can lead to a disregard for the nuances of different data sets and structures, the inability to respond effectively to changing situations, underutilization of diverse insights from data, and a false sense of security in the supposed predictability afforded by data standards and traditional governance approaches. **The remedy is adaptive management and governance.** Systems must be designed so that people and practices are updated as new data and information is gathered.

#4: The Delusion of Risk Control. This is the erroneous belief that comprehensive rules, procedures, and work systems can entirely eliminate or control risks. It's a particularly compelling delusion because it offers the appealing illusion of security and predictability. But despite their benefits, these systems can inadvertently create new complexities and hazards. For example, perceived control over risks leads to an increase in risky behavior: the safer people believe they are, the more risks they are willing to take because they believe they are well-protected. This can result in new, unforeseen risks. With regard to data and analytics, this delusion could lead to overconfidence in data security protocols, reliability of the infrastructure, or the accuracy of information in reports and on dashboards. **The remedy is to replace certainty with a healthy regard for complexity.** While risk control systems are crucial, it is equally important to recognize their limitations and maintain vigilance against complacency and changing external conditions.

#5: The Delusion of Human Error. This represents a flawed perspective that attributes the majority of failures to human mistakes, and argues that these can be eliminated through behavioral modification (otherwise known as "more training"). It vastly oversimplifies the power of a single person to do something unwanted, while ignoring the much larger role that the work system plays in determining the likelihood that an error will arise in the first place. This delusion erroneously frames human error as a cause, rather than a symptom, of flaws in a work system. In data and analytics, this can manifest as multiple values being calculated for the same metric, like customer satisfaction or a revenue forecast. **The remedy is to build competency.** For example, instead of training people to be data literate in general and providing them with a self-service smorgasbord of all business objects and metrics in the company, help them build specific competencies around forming insights that are relevant to their roles.

#6: The Delusion of Quantification. This is the belief that performance can be adequately represented through metrics at all. Recognizing that anyone can misrepresent or manipulate data to meet goals or to avoid negative attention, this delusion can lead to a range of detrimental behaviors, such as limiting reporting to meet targets, thereby making the data unreliable and invalid. This may manifest as an overreliance on simplistic metrics that do not accurately represent the complex, multi-dimensional nature of risks and issues. If you're not measuring the right things, your measurements are meaningless as management tools. In safety management, a goal of "zero incidents" can lead to a range of organizational failures. This includes a zero tolerance approach that treats normal system variability as abnormal, and suppresses reporting of mistakes, risks, and potential problems. (Do you know anyone who throws out "outliers" without checking to see if they're physically valid measurements?) **The remedy is to understand and embrace variability.** Abandon unrealistic expectations of achieving perfect order and zero errors, and establish defenses against the illusion of perfection, which will open up opportunities for learning and improvement. Continually improving any complex system is never a journey with a decisive victory at the end.

#7: The Delusion of Invulnerability. This is the mindset or culture where a person or an organization is either ignorant of - perceives itself to be *immune to* - accidents, errors, or failures. This delusion can become embedded in an organization when people gain a false sense of security from rigorous compliance, from low incident rates that reinforce this belief, from successful heroic efforts that have reduced the urgency to attend to root cause issues, or from withholding evidence due to a conviction that quality is "just fine". The drive towards achieving targets, coupled with the pressure to maintain the appearance of infallibility, can lead individuals to conceal risks or cover up issues, thus exacerbating the delusion. **The remedy is to build resilience.** Be open to the data and analytics that remind you of your vulnerability, because they will keep you on an honest path of awareness and improvement.

There's one final delusion that's rarely called out: that all you need is to "hire good people" and then "trust your team" - two dangerous delusions that shift the burden of success away from the work system and its managers, to the people who have to work within that system. Any organization can hire great people with strong individual skill sets, but few can create work systems that efficiently and effectively harness the power of teams. Even if a team is fully populated with great, highly skilled, well-intentioned people, it can be fully dysfunctional when it attempts to work together. By carefully crafting work systems, organizations can help its people resist and avoid the delusions that breed overconfidence and danger.

TIME TRAVEL WITH STANDARDS

The delusions show us that prescriptive guidance is necessary, *but not sufficient*, to grow a culture of safety and performance. While standards and regulations are sometimes perceived as unnecessary bureaucracy, they are critical conduits for rich contextual information.

Every rule exists because something bad, unexpected, or undesirable happened in the past. Rather than feeling dismayed or overwhelmed by standards or regulations, think of them as time travel: they are messages, containing critical data information from your predecessors. They want you to avoid the negative consequences they had to experience.

Bob Lauder, who worked on Piper Alpha between 1978 and 1980 (and who retired from his position as Health and Safety Manager with Oil & Gas UK in 2018), remarked in a 2018 interview that as older workers retire, the memory of the disaster is fading. "The fact remains, however, that the lessons learned from Piper Alpha have been embedded into our legislation and management systems and have helped shape the current industry safety culture... that offers some assurance that the lessons from Piper are transferred across generations and that the legacy arrangements are effective in managing major accident hazards." (Boman 2018)

DIGITAL DIRECTIONS

Digital technology has immense potential to enhance the performance of any business process, but in particular, safety and emergency preparedness. This is where the stakes are *literally* life and death. This performance improvement occurs by improving the exchange of accurate and timely data by fostering connectedness, increasing intelligence, and automating connections between systems. (Radziwill 2020)

Piper Alpha survivor Steve Rae (2018) suggested many options for using data, analytics, and digital technologies to achieve a paradigm shift in safety, building competencies and mastery in rich ways. One approach is to leverage remote assessment and coaching. Skilled mentors can pair with a connected worker, using real-time body cameras or video technology, to observe and guide workers in their respective environments.

Immediate feedback like this can lead to improved performance and increased adherence to safety practices and principles, while helping workers develop a sensitivity to know when to take an intelligent risk and deviate. Smart headsets and visors can provide visual and audio guidance at the point of use for any piece of equipment or machinery, ensuring that instructions are timely, context-specific, and easily accessible to the worker. This can increase the likelihood of safe behaviors.

Context-aware tools and artificial intelligence can offer real-time monitoring and control of workflows at remote sites, mimicking the advancements seen in onshore manufacturing facilities. Situational awareness coaching can be enhanced with augmented reality and virtual reality to help workers recognize danger zones and alerts them when they're at risk. These technologies can also recommend actions to take so preventive maintenance can protect from potential failures.

"Model and magic are both 5-letter words that start with M.
*The important thing is to understand the **difference**."*
– T. Scott Clendaniel, VP of AI at Analytics Edge

Leveraging intelligent and automated systems not only enhances safety but can also boost productivity and efficiency. Integrating data-rich digital technologies to directly support the workforce *in situ* can revolutionize safety management, making it more proactive, personalized, and effective.

THE BOTTOM LINE

Every process failure shines the light on an opportunity for improvement around data or analytics... meaning that data and analytics can help you *debug your business*. This is because incidents occur when people or systems don't have the right information (of the right quality) in time to prevent the failure. Major industrial accidents and research in safety management provides a powerful lens to see how the seven types of delusion can lead to complacency, and how data and analytics can be used to pierce unfounded confidence.

*"Data and analytics help you **debug your business**."*
– Ergest Xheblati, Data Expert

An effective data strategy to support any critical process must ask one key question. How can we ensure that data and information of the appropriate quality gets to the people and systems that need it *in time* for them to make the decisions that will protect the integrity of a process... thus protecting the people who support it?

For situations that involve safety, we ask: how can we ensure that accurate and complete information gets to the people and systems that need it *in time* for them to make decisions that will protect the integrity of machinery and equipment, and keep the people who use it safe? To round out the strategy, embed this information flow within a systematic approach to managing the process, keeping accountability close to those who are closest to the work and in control of the outcomes.

Withholding data and information, and failing to detect and act on early warnings, can lead to missed opportunities for improvement that lead to injuries and death. Delusion emerges in the whitespace of how people relate to each other in groups, and breeds confidence because it feels so certain. To combat the dominant narratives, surround yourself with data, analytics, and *people* that will challenge you.

REFERENCES

Appleton, Sir Brian. (2013, August 1). Piper Alpha Accident. *BBC*. Available from https://www.youtube.com/watch?v=S9h8MKG88_U

Boman, K. (2018, June 18). Piper Alpha 30th anniversary: Industry must not let complacency set in, lessons learned be forgotten. *Drilling Contractor*. Available from https://drillingcontractor.org/piper-alpha-30th-anniversary-industry-must-not-let-complacency-set-in-lessons-learned-be-forgotten-47377

MacLeod, F. & Richardson, S. (2018, July 6). Piper Alpha: The Disaster in Detail. *Chemical Engineer*. Available from https://www.thechemicalengineer.com/features/piper-alpha-the-disaster-in-detail/

Pitzer, C. (2016). The Great Swindles, Scams, and Myths in Safety. White Paper. Available from https://www.smenet.org/docs/public/Gen-CorriePitzer-Paper_072016.pdf

Radziwill, N. (2020). Connected, intelligent, automated: The definitive guide to digital transformation and quality 4.0. ASQ Quality Press, Milwaukee WI.

Rae, S. (2018, July 3). Steve Rae: Piper Alpha Survivor. *Chemical Engineer.* Available from https://www.thechemicalengineer.com/features/steve-rae-piper-alpha-survivor/

Reason, J. (2016). Managing the risks of organizational accidents. Routledge.

Shallcross, D. C. (2013). Using concept maps to assess learning of safety case studies – The Piper Alpha disaster. *Education for Chemical Engineers*, 8(1), e1-e11.

PART II:

BUILDING A FOUNDATION
FOR TRUST

DATA QUALITY

LOSSY | LOSSLESS

| SOMEONE WHO ONCE SAW THE DATA DESCRIBING IT AT A PARTY | BLOOM FILTER | HASH TABLE | JPEG, GIF MPEG | PNG, ZIP, TIFF, WAV, RAW DATA | RAW DATA + PARITY BITS FOR ERROR DETECTION | RAW DATA + PARITY BITS FOR ERROR CORRECTION | BETTER DATA |

https://xkcd.com/2739/

CHAPTER 5

DATA INTEGRITY IS PROCESS INTEGRITY

"Our plans are measured in centuries."
-- Reverend Mother Mohiam of the Bene Gesserit in Dune

In February 2024, thousands of publicly traded businesses started the process of reporting their final earnings for the last quarter of 2023. Among them was ride-sharing company Lyft. While the year had been somewhat profitable for Lyft, their financials weren't particularly noteworthy. The company was still struggling to become consistently profitable.

But two days later, investors were not only excited about Lyft, but in a *frenzy* to buy. Why? The earnings release that had been shared with the public reported a *five percent increase* in adjusted earnings (EBITDA) instead of the real increase of only half a percent. That's a big difference! But it wasn't as exciting as they had hoped. Somehow, an extra zero had been tacked onto a number in the report, over-reporting revenue by a factor of ten. Buoyed by the error, Lyft's stock soared 67%. (Noto 2024)

The CEO shifted into damage control mode quickly, appearing on network news shows to claim sole responsibility for the error and apologize to the public. (After the panic subsided, the stock price maintained half of its gain prior to the CEO's apology, so it's unclear just how unlucky the error might *actually* have been for the company and its investors.)

While opinions differ around what happened or how it happened, everyone at Lyft converged around a single story: it was a "clerical error." But that makes it sound like a single person was at fault. (In the week after this, the internet was abuzz, trying to figure out *who got fired* for the drama. It's not uncommon for front line employees to be the "heads that roll" when external failures have the potential to damage reputations.)

But even the *smallest* of typos reflect failure modes in a *process*. Whoever typed the numbers into the press release had to have retrieved them from a dashboard, report, or other internal asset. (Who knows just how many dashboards or reports that public relations person had available to choose from, or just how many different queries were in place to pull information.) In all cases, a process brings many people together to pursue a common objective - whether those people are aware of each other or not.

PROCESS INTEGRITY AND INSIDER TRADING

The Lyft example is not an outlier: real-time data and news feeds *typically* drive after hours stock market trading. While their amazing revenue numbers were an accident, perception can be manipulated to yield results that can be just as spectacular.

In 2011, the Long Island Iced Tea Corporation set out on a mission: to bring non-alcoholic ready-to-drink iced teas and lemonades to the most discerning of beverage consumers. By leveraging the iconic name of the popular (and strong) alcoholic drink, and its headquarters address in Hicksville, New York, they were bound to get instant attention. What could go wrong?

The business experienced healthy growth, but *never quite* got to the level that the company's leaders desired. But 2016 turned out to be a transformative year thanks to the cryptocurrency Bitcoin, and the mystique of the blockchain driving it. In February 2017, the price of Bitcoin surged over $1,000, marking its graduation from "prototype technology" to potentially lucrative asset. On December 15, 2017, Bitcoin hit $19,650, creating a new cohort of millionaires and billionaires. Around the same time, the Securities and Exchange Commission (SEC) notified the iced tea vendors that they had a big problem to solve: get above the $35M revenue threshold or risk being delisted.

Since piggybacking on the name of a popular alcoholic beverage had been good for business, *why not leverage the power of blockchain to catapult sales to the next level?* The company went all in on their bet, rebranding their operation in December 2017 as The Long Blockchain Corporation, and trading under LBCC on the New York Stock Exchange.

It was excellent timing: Bitcoin frenzy had not even started to peak. Analysts at the time were predicting a $100K Bitcoin price by the end of 2018, and tens of thousands of people were rushing to buy Bitcoin and Bitcoin-related stock... including LBCC. Many, in the excitement of the gold rush, were probably not even aware that they were only investing in gold-colored beverages.

The bet paid off: trading volume, and the LBCC share price, zoomed upwards by 1000%. Excitement was palpable, inside and outside the booming company. Unfortunately, the excitement was just a little bit premature. A couple days before the LBCC announcement, one of the company's shareholders sent a draft press release to a stockholder friend, who happened to mention the upcoming rebranding to someone else... who immediately recognized the potential payoff of the marketing decision. That friend-of-a-friend bought 35,000 shares right before the price surge, and sold them a few hours afterwards at a profit of $160K.

Unfortunately, insider trading is illegal, and in addition to sanctions on the individuals who participated (knowingly or unknowingly) in the scheme, the stock exchange delisted LBCC. (Egan, 2018)

EVEN SIMPLE DATA REQUIRES SOLID PROCESS

Quality cost studies tell us that failures impacting customers are *many times more costly and damaging* than failures that only impact employees. In the Lyft case, layers of quality controls weren't sufficient to prevent an expensive global misunderstanding. In the LBCC case, insiders manipulated shared understanding to achieve a dubious alignment around perception of the company's offerings and share value. But even the simplest data requires process integrity.

To gain process integrity, focus on building *shared understanding* and gaining *alignment*. Because processes can span organizational boundaries, this starts with articulating the process (translation: just write it down!) Years ago, one of my teams worked with a government agency on a process that took 157 days from start to finish. We got all the stakeholders around a whiteboard, and without using *any* advanced techniques, we sketched out the process that connected these people together.

After years of carrying out the process, they were able to see how the different ways individual people *experienced* the process were getting in the way of successfully completing it. Later, the team was able to identify changes to the process that removed additional bottlenecks and delays. By pursuing shared understanding and alignment, they shortened the mean time to complete the process from 157 days to 21 days.

At another mid-market ecommerce company, a data team got

a seemingly simple request: find out why the number of orders on one report differed from the number of orders on a second report. (Counting orders should be simple, especially when a company's viability depends on bringing in orders!) The analysts traced the data lineage of the order counting process through five dashboards that delivered those values to users and found that *all* the dashboards were wrong: each business unit that added to the order tally counted them in *different ways*. One unit only counted an order if it hadn't been canceled or refunded within 24 hours. Another unit counted *all* orders, even the ones that failed in real-time due to website errors. Yet another unit waited up to a week until the funds were captured, crediting the order one or more days after the customer placed it.

Counting orders was a challenge because of the lack of *process integrity*: each team generated orders in completely different ways. Their organizations failed to build shared understanding around what it meant to *be* an order, and the conditions for a request for products or services to officially become an order. To solve the data quality problem, it would be necessary to *solve the process quality problem first*.

PROCESS INTEGRITY REQUIRES ALIGNMENT

The second element of process integrity is alignment, that is, making sure a process is "seamless" and that the intentions of each contributor agree with one another. Agreement requires leveraging the power of the network of people. Here's an example.

How many times have you received a sales pitch online, but don't click through to find out more because you don't want to be spammed multiple times a week by a company's most junior business development reps?

How many messages do you get every week on LinkedIn that sound like this, completely misaligned with the kind of outreach that might make you feel comfortable connecting?

```
Hi [First Name],

I am reaching out to see if we can schedule a meeting
to discuss how we can potentially work together.

We specialize in lead generation and appointment-
setting programs, and I believe that our expertise
could be of great benefit to your company. Please let
me know if this is something that interests you.

Are you open for a brief discussion this week? Please
book your schedule preference here: [my Calendly]

Thanks and I look forward to hearing from you.

Best regards,

[Someone you've never heard of before]
[Some company you've never heard of before]
```

If messages like this irritate you, you're not alone. You're picking up on *a misalignment* between marketing and sales functions in the company that approached you. While you might benefit from the service the rep is trying to pitch, you're a busy person who is unlikely to have a spare half hour to invest in a vague promise. It's a big turn-off.

This dynamic plays out over and over: while sales is sweating to convert leads to opportunities and close deals, marketing unintentionally chases leads away. According to Justin Shriber, a former VP of Marketing at LinkedIn, "Marketing and Sales teams waste an estimated $1 trillion dollars per year due to a lack of coordination" in the U.S. alone. Why?

- Marketing reps don't understand the sales process, or

what is needed to close deals.

- Sales reps don't completely understand the product.

This example shows how shared understanding and alignment are deeply intertwined. Misalignment can be fixed, and the degree of alignment can be measured and continuously improved. Alignment is the *best* way to reduce friction (between people, and between people and systems) to accelerate *real* progress towards tangible goals.

SYMPTOMS OF MISALIGNMENT

Does your team have alignment issues? They can be diagnosed by watching how people work, and taking the emotional temperature of a team's members: Are any of the following conditions present?

- **Vague Feelings of Fear.** Your organization has a strategic plan (knows WHAT it wants to do), but there is little to no coordination regarding HOW people across the organization will accomplish strategic objectives. You know what KPIs you're supposed to deliver on, but you don't know how exactly you're supposed to work with anything in your power or control to "move the needle."

- **Ivory Tower Syndrome.** You're in a meeting and get the visceral sense that things aren't clear, or that different people have different expectations for a project or initiative. But you're too nervous or uncertain to ask for clarification – or maybe you do ask, but you get an equally unclear answer. Naturally, you assume that everyone in the room is smarter than you (particularly the managers) so you shut up and hope that it makes sense later. The reality is that you may be picking up on a legitimate problem that's going to be problematic for the organization later.

- **Surprises.** A department committed you to a task, but you weren't part of that decision. Once you find out about it, the task just may not get done. Alternatively, you'll have to adjust your workload and reset expectations with the stakeholders who will now be disappointed that you can't meet their needs according to the original schedule. Or maybe work evenings and weekends to get the job done on time. Either way, it's not pleasant for anyone.

- **Emergencies**. How often are you called on to respond to something that's absolutely needed by the close of business today? How often are you expected to drop everything and take care of it? How often do you have to work nights and weekends to make sure you don't fall behind?

- **Lead Balloons.** In this scenario, key stakeholders are called into projects at the 11th hour, when they are unable to guide or influence the direction of an initiative. The initiative becomes a "dead man walking" that's doomed to an untimely end, but since the organization has sunk time and effort into it, people will push ahead anyway.

- **Cut Off at the Pass.** Have you ever been working on a project and found out – somewhere in the middle of doing it – that some other person or team has been working on the same thing? Or maybe they've been working on a different project, but it's ultimately at cross purposes with yours. Whatever way this situation works out, your organization ends up with a pile of waste and potential rework.

- **Not Writing Things Down.** It's important to make sure everyone is literally on the same page, seeing the world in a similar enough way to know they are pursuing the same goals and objectives. If you don't write things down, you may be at the mercy of cognitive biases later. How do you know that your goals and objectives are aligned with your overall company strategy? Can you review written minutes after key meetings? Are your organization's strategic initiatives written and agreed to by decision makers? Do you implement project charters that all stakeholders are required to sign off on before work can commence? What practices do you use to get everyone on the same page?

Lack of alignment negatively impacts outcomes, professional relationships, and ultimately the bottom line. It can emerge between *any* two people or process steps. A January 2018 survey from software company Altify specifically looked at diagnosing misalignment between sales and marketing functions. This is significant because sales teams use marketing collateral to understand products or services. In total, 422 enterprise-level executives and sales leaders surveyed revealed:

- 74% of marketers think they understood customer needs, but only 44% of salespeople in their organizations agreed

- 71% of marketers think sales and marketing are aligned, but only 59% of salespeople in their organizations agreed

Subtle as they may appear, these discrepancies expose a misalignment between the sales and marketing departments. One group believes they have a firm grasp of the situation, while members of the other group silently disagree. This diagnostic approach can be equally applied to assess the alignment between two people.

DATA INTEGRITY & PSYCHOLOGICAL SAFETY

Organizations can't expect to achieve data integrity without psychological safety. Improving psychological safety requires inclusive practices, first and foremost to ensure access to physical, informational, and social resources at both the team and organizational levels. (Radziwill & Benton, 2024) When employees feel valued, respected, and supported, they are more likely to contribute openly and honestly, which is essential for maintaining data integrity. Everyone must be comfortable speaking up about data issues, errors, or inconsistencies without fear of negative consequences.

This means data integrity is a team sport. Whenever a team member is afraid to raise concerns or work through errors, data integrity can be compromised, compounding inaccurate insights and leading to poor decision-making over time.

"Leaders who don't listen to their teams will eventually find themselves with
teams who have nothing to say."
-- Leila Hormozi, CEO of acquisition.com

At Vale S.A., the world's largest iron ore producer, the lack of psychological safety led to disastrous consequences. Despite the company's public commitment to sustainability and environmental protection, an investigation by the U.S. Securities and Exchange Commission (SEC) after a catastrophic tailings dam failure in 2019 revealed that Vale had knowingly misled investors about the safety and stability of its dams. Vale's Environmental, Social & Governance (ESG) data had been misreported for years prior to the catastrophe, fueled by fear at all levels of the organization. (Radziwill 2023)

Fear is a silencer. Workers in this case would have been more likely to report accurate data and raise concerns about potential issues if they had no fear of retaliation or negative consequences.

In Vale's case, if employees had felt comfortable reporting the true state of the tailings dams, and if their managers had not been afraid to escalate, the company might have taken appropriate action to address the safety concerns, preventing damages and deaths. Employees may have felt pressured to present a positive image of the company's sustainability efforts by falsifying ESG data. This case underscores how fostering a culture of psychological safety will protect data integrity - and can even protect life and property.

THE OFFICE IS A MICROCOSM OF SOCIETY

In my 20's, I was convinced that once I got enough education and experience, any workplace I'd be a part of would run smoothly. What I didn't realize in these early years of my career was that *there is no utopian work environment*. Regardless of how skilled or experienced I personally might become, there is no workplace where *everyone* will be educated enough, competent enough, informed enough, and emotionally healthy enough - all the time - for interactions to be completely productive and frictionless.

To compound this calculation, people routinely move in and out of organizations. They are hired, do work, get promoted or reassigned, retire, and are fired. Each of these personnel actions also impacts the workers around the affected individual, changing the fabric of relationships for good or ill. These people have been indelibly impacted by how they were treated in past work experiences, and the degree to which they observed fairness and kindness expressed to others. There are early career people, later career people, and others who are practicing new (to them) skills. Everyone is learning, all the time, whether it feels like it or not.

Not everyone will be happy or content at every moment, and every workplace will be toxic... for *somebody*. As a result, to achieve alignment, we must acknowledge that there is tremendous and unending variation in the people that comprise a workforce. We have to work with the variation between people, and the variation within individuals over time, acknowledging the ebb and flow of competencies, attitudes, and challenges.

Someone will be "broken" all the time, and that's part of life. Achieving alignment requires us to design for this variation rather than pretend it doesn't exist.

MAKE A COURAGEOUS INVESTMENT

Like a champion rowing team, your organization needs to make sure *enough* people (in the right roles) are working together, synchronized, actively communicating and collaborating, not working at cross-purposes. But dedicating time to work on alignment can seem like a luxury. With so many urgent business needs to attend to, who can risk slowing down to work on alignment? And besides, alignment just happens naturally when you've hired the best people... right?

> *"Leadership in a quality culture isn't about enforcing rules. It's about **inspiring a shared vision** where quality is everyone's business."*
> *– Harsh Thakkar, CEO of Qualtivate*

Unfortunately, no. Synchronizing people and processes, and making sure everyone is aware of the needs and desires of *real* customers and stakeholders, takes dedicated effort and a commitment from senior leaders. That means sacrificing some of the urgency leaders may feel pressure to answer, and committing to the hard work of building habits and practices that are sustained even as people join and leave the company.

THE BOTTOM LINE

Data integrity is impossible without process integrity. Process integrity requires collaboration and alignment across multiple functional units of a business, and between key people therein. Collaboration requires connection.

"It's no longer sufficient to 'hire the best'.
*You must **hire and wire!**"*
– Valdis Krebs, Network Expert, in Managing the 21st Century Organization (2007)

Every business will have silos, which emerge when people are fearful, are in competition with one another, or otherwise feel as if they have to suppress communications. As a result, every silo gives you clues about where power dynamics have led to this result over time. While people move on from jobs, the silos remain, giving us a hint about where power dynamics were active in the past. Consequently, process integrity is usually harder to achieve (and takes longer to achieve) because of the need to negotiate solutions across silos.

To achieve data integrity, work on strengthening the processes that produce data. This includes probing the relationships and power dynamics of the participants in those processes. Power differentials can make people more guarded in their interactions with each other, leading to silos that must be decommissioned for data to flow effectively. Silos reduce physical, informational, and social access to knowledge and resources, making it hard for people to understand and manage processes together.

Where fear *grows*, potential failure *goes*. Inclusive practices, in contrast, can help bridge the gaps between people that lead to silos and data integrity issues. Establishing the habits and practices that promote process integrity requires designing for the long term, with a vision that extends far beyond the immediate future. Just as the Bene Gesserit in Dune measured their plans in centuries, organizations will benefit from taking a strategic, forward-thinking, longer time duration approach to growing a culture of psychological safety and data integrity that will endure and evolve over time.

"Any time you're operating in a system that's not made for you, it can be traumatizing."
– Daniella Mestyanek Young, Author/childhood cult survivor/commissioned military officer

---

REFERENCES

Egan, M. (2021, July 10). Insider trading charges filed over Long Island Iced Tea's blockchain 'pivot'. *CNN Business*. Available from https://www.cnn.com/2021/07/10/investing/blockchain-long-island-insider-trading/index.html

Krebs, V. (2007). Managing the 21st century organization. HRIM Journal, 11(4), 2-8.

Lyft (2024, February 13). Lyft Announces Fourth Quarter and Full-Year 2023 Results. *Press Release*. Available from https://investor.lyft.com/news-and-events/news/news-details/2024/Lyft-Announces-Fourth-Quarter-and-Full-Year-2023-Results/default.aspx

Noto, G. (2024, February 14). Lyft shares rise 35% after earnings report typo sparks confusion. Available from https://www.cfodive.com/news/lyft-shares-slump-following-cfo-margin-correction/707557

Radziwill, N.M. (2023). Quality-Driven ESG: Build Trust by Improving Data Quality. *Intelex Insight Report*. Available from https://www.intelex.com/resources/insight-report/quality-driven-esg-build-trust-by-improving-data-quality/

Radziwill, N.M. & Benton, M.C. (2024).Inclusion by Design: 8 Actionable Elements for Productive Teaming. *Forthcoming.*

CHAPTER 6

KNOWING WHAT "GOOD" MEANS

"Do not underestimate the power of good data. If you want to take advantage of new AI capabilities, AI eats data for breakfast, lunch and dinner. Make sure you are powering AI with good clean vegetables.."
- Cara Dailey, Chief Data Officer at T. Rowe Price

On June 9, 2023, the popular and prestigious publication *Scientific American* released an article that felt a little different than any of the others in its 178 year history. Bad data, the article's title proclaimed, *not aliens*, may be behind the recent UFO surge.

The author was referring to statistics from 2022, gathered by the U.S. Office of the Director of National Intelligence, on nearly 400 new reports observed mostly by U.S. Navy and U.S. Air Force pilots and personnel. The increase in reports of Unidentified Aerial Phenomena (UAP), the modern and more scientific term for UFOs prior to the National Defense Authorization Act's revision of the acronym to "Unidentified Anomalous Phenomena", is stark when compared to the 144 total reports that were made from 2004 to 2021. (Watson, 2023)

Does this mean Earth is under attack? Of course not. Several reports have proven to be drones, operated by hobbyists who don't realize they need permission to fly into certain areas or altitudes. And in contrast with previous decades, the article states, professionals are less hesitant to make reports, which means more reports will be logged. More people agree that *something* is going on that needs to be understood. While it might not be extraterrestrial, people could be getting glimpses of new surveillance technology invented for military purposes by other countries. Understanding the nature and source of these UAPs is a problem worth investigating.

In addition to the potentially existential threat that could be posed by a legion of otherworldly beings joining our planet, there's a much more practical pain point: *UFOs take up air space*, and like space junk, can pose a risk to the aircraft and air operations that support economies around the globe. We need good data on what's traveling or floating through airspace to protect people, and cargo from adverse incidents, and to protect the integrity of national boundaries.

This is why, in 2022, the U.S. National Aeronautics and Space Administration (NASA) convened the Unidentified Anomalous Phenomena Independent Study Team, to "identify how data gathered by civilian government entities, commercial data, and data from other sources can potentially be analyzed to shed light on UAPs." (NASA, 2022) I've worked with several of the 16 panelists during the 2000's when I led data management and software development at a national lab, and can vouch for their integrity as scientists and connoisseurs of data.

IS SOME DATA BETTER THAN NO DATA?

I was particularly surprised to see *Scientific American* blaming a glut of UFO reports on "bad data" so prominently, right in the title of its article. NASA's own UAP team, in its FAQ, firmly placed the blame on *limited* data, though, *not* bad data: "Most UAP sightings result in very limited data, making it difficult to draw scientific conclusions about the nature of UAP." After all, most of the observations the Director of National Intelligence receives are verbal descriptions of a sighting, metadata about the sighting (like time, place, and direction of view), and sometimes photos or videos from a mobile phone.

Having a *little bit of data* is not the same problem, and often not as significant a problem, as having *bad data* in any volume. We *can* use small samples of data to support inferences about the physical phenomena we're observing, and as long as the data is reasonably good, our findings may be realistic. We may not be confident about our conclusions, but conclusions can be drawn. In contrast, when data is bad, insights made using that data could only be valid *by chance*.

In the case of the mysterious flying objects, more and *better* data are needed. On May 31, 2023, NASA's UAP panel provided an update to reinforce this message. Chair David Spergel, President of the Simons Foundation, explained their rather ordinary initial findings: "Today's existing data and eyewitness reports are insufficient to yield conclusive evidence about the nature and origin of every UAP event, he said, primarily because of a lack of quality control and poor data curation." Simply put, NASA has no way of knowing whether the people and instruments generating the data are trustworthy, and the data they receive can't be expected to come from collections that are systematically organized and maintained.

The *Scientific American* article also calls out the critical need for making sure people interpreting data use the same terminology to understand that data. In the case of the UAPs, determining what is (and is not) anomalous requires knowing what anomalous even *means*: "Gaining any new clarity about surging reports of unidentified anomalous phenomena, or UAP, will take time, better data gathering and diagnostic tools and, perhaps most importantly, a hale and hearty dose of nit-picking scientific scrutiny. It may also require a better, sharper definition of what 'anomalous' even means in the context of recent sightings."

While you'll hear people say "some data is better than no data," in reality, a limited amount of data may either prove useless or misleading. Think about the years of photographs of the Loch Ness Monster, or the grainy images and videos of Bigfoot that inspired curiosity, wonder, and conspiracy theories. Has limited data been useful in these contexts? It hasn't been useful in supporting or denying the existence of the creatures, but it has been useful to catalyze fear and inspiration. Only time will reveal whether the phenomena are real or imagined. It takes reflection, scrutiny, multiple observers and multiple observations to convert data to the information and insights people broadly trust.

WHAT IS DATA, ANYWAY?

You might be wrinkling your brow right now. Those grainy 1967 films of Bigfoot captured by Roger Patterson and Bob Gimlin, those are *data*? In short, yes. The word data, sometimes defined as *"pieces of information"* comes from the Latin *datum*, which means "something that is given." Each element of data is given as a potential clue in a larger problem context.

By giving form or character to data, we bring the given pieces together to generate *information*. If the information passes tests for accuracy and relevance (and maybe other factors, like timeliness), it becomes *evidence*. By aggregating evidence, we can assess the quality of the information in the context of a scenario or decision making challenge. (Bovee et al. 2003) Every alleged Bigfoot video is one potential piece of a puzzle that might help us reveal the truths around the phenomenon *and* the observation... eventually.

Data does not have to be true or verifiable to be considered "data". Consider, for example, a survey on color perception between people with ordinary sight and people who are color blind. Each respondent is given a collection of color swatches, and is asked to report which color they see, selecting from a list of ten options. An honest respondent who is color blind will report different "colors" than an honest respondent who is not color blind. A disengaged respondent might just check some boxes, not paying attention to the link between their personal experience and the data they record, or not caring whether their representation is accurate.

But there's another possibility too. This is one you're *undoubtedly* familiar with.

PEOPLE MAKE STUFF UP

On September 18, 2015, the U.S. Environmental Protection Agency (EPA) accused auto manufacturer Volkswagen of violating the Clean Air Act on a massive scale. According to the allegation, up to 11 million diesel vehicles had been equipped with "defeat software" that would allow them to pass emissions tests at vehicle inspection stations or in labs, while nitrogen oxide continued to pour out at (in some cases) more than 40 times the legal limit. After a lengthy investigation (and excessive resistance and denial by the company) the allegations were ultimately deemed true, Volkswagen (VW) was fined several million dollars, and the C-suite roster was quickly refreshed. (Zhang et al., 2016)

Why would such a well-established company, especially one poised to receive prestigious international awards for corporate social responsibility (CSR), not just lie... but *develop software to lie on its behalf?* Jack Ewing, a reporter who published the full-length book *Faster, Higher, Farther: The Volkswagen Scandal* in 2017, explains the power dynamics that created the conditions for the scandal *over eight decades*. Immediately after World War II, the Porsche and Piëch families who ran the company made a deal with the government and the workers. It essentially shut off any requirement for external oversight, including from shareholders, and enabled an insular, dictatorial corporate climate to emerge.

Did the sanctions lead to culture change at the top of VW? "They talk about creating a new company culture [where evidence and truth are honored]," Ewing explained, "[but] this is still an issue more than a year and a half after it first came to light. And it really shouldn't be. With better crisis management they could have put this behind them in six months or so. But they would have had to make a lot more changes than they were willing to." (Clairmont, 2017)

Over decades, the company had developed a culture and competency around skillfully talking without walking the walk. Many of our organizations do the same, and while the cost of chaos is striking, it's often realized well after the people who allow the chaos to proliferate have left. But the time between misrepresenting reality and having it discovered can be much shorter. "The [VW] case findings illustrate that CSR may become a risk if organizations are not able to fulfill their promises." (Zhang et al., 2016)

"NO INTENTIONAL MISCONDUCT"

Saving time and making money are two reasons that can powerfully motivate some people to fabricate data and information. Consider the case of attorney Steven A. Schwartz of Levidow, Levidow & Oberman in New York City. Schwartz, representing a personal injury case in 2023 for a man whose knee was damaged by a beverage cart on an Avianca Airlines flight to

New York from El Salvador, says that he "heard about this new site, which I falsely assumed was, like, a super search engine." (Weiser & Schweber, 2023)

Just a few queries to ChatGPT, the AI large language model that produces solid and compelling text from questions and other prompts, and Schwartz had a complete legal brief in his hands - in minutes, rather than the days it would usually take. The brief also, however, was based on "more than half a dozen" completely made up case citations. The ChatGPT output sounded *so* good, Schwartz didn't question its origins.

One judge in Texas has decided to preempt similar issues in his courtroom by requiring an affidavit that the attorney vouches for the integrity of a legal brief, and that no AIs were used. "These platforms in their current states are prone to hallucinations and bias... they make stuff up — even quotes and citations... While attorneys swear an oath to set aside their personal prejudices, biases, and beliefs to faithfully uphold the law and represent their clients, generative artificial intelligence is the product of programming devised by humans who did not have to swear such an oath." (Cerullo, 2023)

Schwartz, now referred to as the "ChatGPT lawyer" in some news articles, filed a declaration to assist in his defense. "I did not comprehend that ChatGPT could fabricate cases," he told the judge. His lawyers have asked the judge to be lenient, on the basis that there was "no intentional misconduct" although this case is sure to set a precedent for responsible use of AI in professions where the integrity of data and information is key.

While Schwartz will have to contend with sanctions, those will be temporary. He may *never* be able to shake his new title as patron saint of embarrassing decisions made with AI, no matter how much genuine contrition he has.

UNINTENDED CONSEQUENCES

While many of us don't completely trust the data available to us, trusting data *too much* can have disastrous consequences. Religion is the biggest revenue producing industry in India, and immediately after powerful Generative Pre-trained Transformer (GPT) engines became available for broader use in early 2023, innovation began to flourish. Not one, but *many* AI chatbots to interpret the Bhagavad Gita, the Hindu scripture, appeared.

There was only one problem: interpreting religious scriptures of any kind has never been easy (or automatable). People attach strong emotions to the interpretations that resonate the most personally. In fact, historically, sects and cults have emerged when the differences become too great for people to bear. When AI language models were applied to the problem, people immediately began asking religious scripture bots for advice and instruction. Unfortunately, recommendations from the bots were often scripturally inaccurate, frequently unethical, and sometimes... violent.

Generative AI based on large language models produces output that sounds solid and authoritative but may provide unwise advice. Since they are trained on language patterns, human biases or the advancement of social or political agendas through subtle suggestion is always a risk. Viksit Gaur, a technology executive at Dropbox, reflected on the power that can be accidentally unleashed: "What scares me is that people might interpret this random statistical output as gospel." (Nooreyezdan, 2023)

While taking spiritual advice (or direction) from a bot might seem silly to some of you, I bet you've enthusiastically taken action based on a report or dashboard that contains similarly dubious data and information. Some healthy caution is *always* well advised when you're trying to determine whether data or information is "good".

QUALITY IS IN THE EYE OF THE BEHOLDER

Who gets to decide what "good" data is? One factor that makes data quality challenging is that there are multiple answers to (and perspectives on) this question, and all of them are to some degree valid. There are typically three common roles: the data producer, the data consumer (which can be a person or a system), and the data user. For any given data, there may be a multitude of consumers and users, and even future users whose intentions we can't guess. It can be challenging to get an entire organization aligned around collectively improving data quality because detecting, understanding, and acting on these multiple perspectives is as much an art as it is a science.

The quality of the same data can be judged in completely different ways by data consumers and users. For example, consider three different cases where people or intelligent systems use the same dataset:

- For a **sales executive**, the quality of the data might be primarily assessed on how effectively it can help them meet their own sales goals and objectives. They would be interested in whether customer contact information is accurate, and if historical sales transactions are complete. They might prioritize data that helps identify potential leads, track customer interactions, and measure sales performance. Their determination of data quality would depend on whether it could be used to drive sales growth and generate insights to help them sell to the right prospects at the right time.

- A **software engineer** might evaluate the quality of the same dataset in a purely technical way. They would be concerned with the validity of the format, consistency with other data sources, and whether the format can be ingested by the software systems or algorithms that will consume the data. The engineer might assess whether the data conforms to defined data models or schemas, and check for anomalies or errors that could impact the functionality of software that uses the data. Quality checks would ensure that the data is clean, well-structured, and suitable for integration.

- For **an AI that requires training data**, evaluating data quality would involve different considerations. For supervised learning, AI would require labeled or annotated data that accurately represents the desired characteristic it needs to learn. The quality of the training data would be based on completeness, validity, relevance, diversity, and its ability to describe real-world scenarios. The data would have to align with the AI's training objectives and effectively capture the patterns and nuances necessary for the AI to generalize and make accurate predictions or decisions.

The organization is responsible for establishing standards and guidelines that align with the particular needs and objectives of the users, ensuring that data quality is evaluated from multiple perspectives and in accordance with criteria that are relevant to those perspectives. But that's the easy part. Doing it consistently, and continually improving as the organization learns, is where managing data for quality can become a competitive advantage.

THROWING THE BABY OUT WITH THE BATHWATER

It's also easy to lose information by erroneously deleting data. Eliminating outliers, or scrubbing for anomalies, should also be done with awareness and caution.

Outliers are data elements that deviate significantly from other related elements. Quantitative outliers often appear at the extremes of the data distribution and may be caused by variability in the data or experimental errors. They could be either very high or very low compared to the rest of the data.

While at first glance, outliers may seem like errors or noise that should be eliminated, they sometimes carry important information about the physical phenomena being observed. Outliers can indicate novel or unexpected behavior or characteristics which can lead to new insights. For example, an outlier could provide clues about an emerging customer behavior or a rare, but critical, system failure. If these outliers were eliminated, the information might be missed, leading to slower responses, suboptimal decisions, or models that don't resolve a feature of interest. In some cases, the presence of outliers in training data can even help improve model performance by making models more robust and capable of handling realistic scenarios.

Not all outliers are informative; some may indeed be due to instrument errors, human errors, system errors, or noise. Instead of simply eliminating outliers, investigate them thoroughly to determine their cause and potential impact on the data and the models built using that data.

THE BOTTOM LINE

You (and your organization) can't be *data driven* until there is sufficient data of high enough quality to *drive you*. While data quality is easy to get wrong, and hard to get right, we still need to build daily habits and practices around good data hygiene. By establishing meaningful measurement systems, we ensure that bad data is not the default excuse when things go wrong, or the scapegoat that absolves all wrongs. *Reaching the point where meaningful insights can inspire and compel action requires time and intentional curation.*

Even when that threshold has been achieved, the human element never goes away. It's just as easy to *mislead with data* as it is to lead with it. There are a multitude of reasons why people might fabricate data and information: to make money, to avoid losing money, to avoid negative consequences, or to avoid extra work. Manipulating or withholding data and information can also support self-preservation or reinforce power over other people. Misleading can be accomplished by falsifying or selectively choosing data, by crafting a seductive or suggestive story, or by using technologies that appear superhuman at first glance (and so remain unchallenged). In the best of cases, distinguishing truth from illusion is difficult; in the most challenging cases, we're our own worst enemies.

To transform through data and become data-driven, we have to consciously adjust habits and practices on many levels: as individuals, as data producers, as data consumers, and as stakeholders. Not all data is created equally, and the quality of *every* data-driven decision depends on data being clean enough, and meaningful enough.

REFERENCES

Bovee, M., Srivastava, R. P., & Mak, B. (2003). A conceptual framework and belief-function approach to assessing overall information quality. *International Journal of Intelligent Systems*, 18(1), 51-74.

Cerullo, M. (2023, June 2). Texas judge bans filings solely created by AI after ChatGPT made up cases. CBS News. Available from https://www.cbsnews.com/news/texas-judge-bans-chatgpt-court-filing/

Clairmont, N. (2017, May 23). Volkswagen's Diesel Scandal Was 80 Years in the Making. *The Atlantic*. Available from https://www.theatlantic.com/business/archive/2017/05/ewing-volkswagen-scandal/527835/

David, Leonard. (2023, June 9). Bad Data, Not Aliens, May Be behind UFO Surge, NASA Team Says. *Scientific American*. Available from https://www.scientificamerican.com/article/bad-data-not-aliens-may-be-behind-ufo-surge-nasa-team-says/

National Aeronautics and Space Administration (NASA). (2022, October 21). NASA Announces Unidentified Anomalous Phenomena Study Team Members. Available from https://www.nasa.gov/feature/nasa-announces-unidentified-anomalous-phenomena-study-team-members/

NASA (2023). Available from https://science.nasa.gov/uap/faqs

Nooreyezdan, N. (2023, May 9). India's religious AI chatbots are speaking in the voice of god — and condoning violence. *Rest of World*. Available from https://restofworld.org/2023/chatgpt-religious-chatbots-india-gitagpt-krishna/

Watson, E. (2023, January 12). Hundreds more UFO sightings included in latest report. *CBS News*. Available from https://www.cbsnews.com/news/hundreds-more-ufo-sightings-included-latest-report/

Weiser, B. & Schweber, N. (2023, June 8). The ChatGPT Lawyer Explains Himself. *New York Times*. Available from https://www.nytimes.com/2023/06/08/nyregion/lawyer-chatgpt-sanctions.html

Zhang, B., Vos, M., Veijalainen, J., Wang, S., & Kotkov, D. (2016). The issue arena of a corporate social responsibility crisis: The Volkswagen case in Twitter. *Studies in Media and Communication*, 4(2).

CHAPTER 7

EVIDENCE, CONTEXT & ACTION

"You've got to know when to hold em
Know when to fold em
Know when to walk away
And know when to run."
-- *Kenny Rogers in* The Gambler *(1978)*

You want to be data-driven. You want your *organization* to be data-driven. While it's rare to encounter someone who will argue *against* becoming data-driven, it's just as rare to find a well-articulated strategy that explains exactly what "data-driven" means (and how you'll know when you achieve it). But the importance of becoming data-driven remains: after all, every disaster movie starts with one data-driven scientist raising flags that mere mortals proceed to ignore.

I was a front row witness to one of these invisible red flags the morning I arrived at the office an unexpected hour early. This gave me the opportunity to sit in on the marketing team's daily standup meeting. I had been helping them understand and interpret the go-to-market plan to more easily find leads in our target markets, so it would be a win-win for me to join in.

But as I rounded the corner, I could already see distress on everyone's faces as the meeting was called to order.

"We got between 1000 and 1200 hits to our web site *every day* last week," the VP of marketing said. "But yesterday, we only had 832. This is *urgent*. We need to redesign the web page *today*," he said. The young, usually vibrant staff nodded with hesitation, resigned to the conclusion dictated from the guy with power.

"I guess we know what *we'll* be doing today," one of the more junior people said, coupled with a long exhale.

"Well at least we're *data driven!!*" a Director exclaimed, sharing a knowing nod with the VP. There was a slight murmur of discomfort, but everyone knew it wasn't appropriate to draw attention away from the action item at hand. The team scurried back to their desks, disbanding into various states of mental health and well-being.

No one challenged the heavy-lift action item: *redesign the web page today*. The decision was, after all, *driven by data*.

REALITY CHECK

If this was a scene in a movie, this is the point that you'd hear the scrubbing sound the DJ makes of the record, or see the video freeze. One of the characters would turn to you, break the fourth wall, and confirm what you were already suspecting: *I don't know what you were thinking, but... this is **not** what it means to be data driven*.

Looking at some numbers and reacting to them may indeed, *literally*, represent you being driven by data (sometimes off a cliff), but that's not the goal. A true data-driven organization values and honors **evidence**, follows processes to interpret the evidence from multiple perspectives within a current **context**, and based on that interpretation, determines whether an **action**

to realize change should be taken now, later, or never. Finally, that action is facilitated, and the organization works to sustain the change.

EVIDENCE → CONTEXT → ACTION

As a data-driven professional, your job is to master the art of assessing the quality of evidence within a given context of interpretation. The remaining step is to find (or create) an environment that's conducive to facilitated action. No matter how data-driven you are as an individual, you'll feel frustrated and lonely if you're surrounded by others who do not share the same values.

EVIDENCE-BASED PRACTICE

The Evidence-Context-Action approach to understanding the data-driven mindset is based on research from a well-established mindset in healthcare: evidence-based practice (EBP). This is known as the conscientious, explicit, and judicious use of current best evidence in making decisions about the care of individual patients. It involves integrating individual expertise with the best available research results. The premise of EBP is that better outcomes result when decisions are informed by reliable and relevant evidence rather than by assumptions, traditions, or anecdotal experiences. (Kitson et al., 1998)

Translating this to a data-driven mindset, EBP would mean combining the unique knowledge, skills, and experiences of professionals in the field with robust and rigorously analyzed data. Just as EBP in healthcare calls for incorporating best research evidence with clinical knowledge and patient values, a data-driven mindset also requires incorporating best data evidence with business acumen and stakeholder values.

To apply EBP to a data-driven mindset, one would start by formulating a clear question or identifying a problem that needs to be solved. Next, they would conduct a thorough search for the best available data relevant to the question. The data must then be rigorously analyzed and critically appraised for its validity, impact, and applicability. Following that, the results must be applied to the decision-making process, taking into account the organizational context and stakeholder values. Lastly, the outcomes of the decision should be evaluated, and the results used to further refine the data-driven process, just as EBP calls for the evaluation of the outcomes of healthcare interventions.

It's also important to gain a healthy perspective on *what is and is not possible* when we use data in an attempt to spur action. We tell ourselves that by presenting the right data, by visualizing it in a compelling way and crafting the right narrative around it, *that's* what will inspire people to action. Logic will prevail. But in reality, many highly skilled data analysts and scientists experience just the opposite: senior leaders and executives who are quick to accept evidence that supports their intuition and desires, but de-emphasize data that does not. These "cherry pickers" can only be countered by leveraging power differentials to impose a higher standard.

DECISION INFRASTRUCTURE

Every business is a data business, each with its own unique decision infrastructure. This is because every business is centered around processes, and all processes can (and should) be described by data. In many enterprises, the data that is needed to define and describe each process is called operational data, while the data and analytics that reflect insights within (or across) processes is called analytical data. No two businesses will have the same processes or technological infrastructure.

"Information is data endowed with relevance and purpose." -- Peter Drucker

This system of interconnected information, the infrastructure upon which all decisions are based, is maintained and evolved by working on three things:

1. **Data Management:** The mechanisms required to acquire, integrate, process, deliver, and *generate value and business impact* through solid decisions.

2. **Data Governance:** The standards and practices adopted by people to *preserve the integrity* of the data and the ecosystem it is embedded within.

3. **Data Strategy:** The longer-term actions needed to continually improve data management and data governance over time to support *novel* insights or *new* capabilities.

The quality of your evidence will depend on the integrity of the data management and data governance processes that generated and maintained it. As a result, to help your organization identify the linkages between data and a value-generating analytics use case, you'll need some insight into the steps that occur when raw data is cleaned and transformed into new information.

But some caution is advised! Identifying all the stops on the data's journey, and finding out *for sure* what happens at each stop, is not a quest for the faint of heart. Due to silos, sluggish communications, clunky technology, technical debt, and current and historical power struggles, the data's journey through an organization's data ecosystem is often clouded by misinformation, misunderstandings, and missing links. But you *still* need to know the data journey to accurately determine the quality and rigor of *any* data or information that you use as evidence.

THE INDUSTRIAL KITCHEN ANALOGY

These concepts can be made more "real" by imagining that your data ecosystem is, instead, an industrial kitchen in a restaurant. If restaurants managed food service like most companies manage and govern their data, the restaurants would be in shambles and people would routinely get sick (or die).

---

*"Quality is to data as organic is to food.
As the raw material of the AI age,
data should be managed by practices that promote
health, integrity and sustainability."*
– Allison Sagraves, Carnegie Mellon CDAIO Faculty

If you're running a restaurant, the notion of customer value is *always* in focus. You want to choose recipes that people are going to enjoy, you want to choose ingredients that are going to make those recipes taste great, and you want to design a production system that gets those recipes delivered to your customers quick enough their nonfunctional requirements are met – like food not being cold when it arrives, and food not making them sick during (or after) their meal.

Using this analogy:

- **"Data Management" in a Kitchen:** The mechanisms required to acquire, prepare, cook, plate, and *generate* *value and business impact* through meals served to customers.

- o The **evidence** (data) includes raw ingredients, cleaned and prepared ingredients, and fully prepared (but not plated) servings. These are combined and arranged with each other to be delivered to customers (usually on plates).

- **"Data Governance" in a Kitchen:** The standards and practices adopted by people to *preserve the integrity* of the ingredients and the system (of procuring, preparing, and serving) that those ingredients are embedded within.
  - o The **context** includes the setting of the restaurant and the expectations the customers have for quality (e.g. fast food vs. fine dining). Kitchens serving fast food may optimize their management processes for speed, while fine dining establishments tend to optimize for product and service quality.

- **"Data Strategy" in a Kitchen:** The longer-term actions needed to continually improve management and governance processes over time to support *new* menu items or *new* capabilities (like take-out).
  - o The **actions** to realize change include training on new methods, exploring new recipes, establishing new processes for controlling the ingredients and their use, and refining the recipes as customer feedback is gathered.

Because the stakes for product quality can literally be life and death, food and beverage is a *highly regulated* industry. Certified inspectors are required to routinely validate all management and governance processes in a restaurant. In contrast, most quality controls and governance mechanisms are optional (that is, not regulated) as data governance programs are constructed (outside financial services and fintech).

EVIDENCE

Using evidence-based practice as a model, we can define **evidence** as reliable data and information that has been rigorously collected and constructed. To count as "evidence" the provenance of the data must be well understood, and it must meet standards for objectivity. Not all raw data will be "evidence quality" but when data has been systematically processed, analyzed, and interpreted, we know we can rely on it to provide insights and inform decision-making.

The quality of evidence depends on:

- **Supplier Qualification:** If some of your data is provided by third party suppliers (or other subsystems managed in some distant part of your organization), the quality of what you receive will depend on the quality assurance processes *they* embrace. Choose them wisely and monitor their quality assurance processes over time.

- **Supplier Quality Assessment:** As you receive data from a supplier, verify that it meets your requirements for data quality on arrival before you store or use it. While the supplier should adhere to solid processes, the data you receive should also be validated and verified.

- **Measurement Systems Analysis:** It is important to know how data is generated at its source. Knowing who or what produced it, when and where it was generated, and why it was collected helps you evaluate the evidence in the context of the decisions you will make.

- **Chain of Custody:** It can be important to keep a chronological record of handoffs and ownership changes to verify the authenticity of the data and confirm that data privacy and security procedures have been followed.

- **The Data Journey:** It is important to know *who* touches data (and what they do to it) as it is cleaned, transformed, and used to generate new knowledge. Every step provides the opportunity to introduce human (and other) errors, so tests at each of these steps can provide quality assurance.

Using the industrial kitchen analogy, imagine how these elements might appear when looking at the "business use case" of your top selling fish dish:

- **Supplier Qualification**: Using a systematic process to make sure every fish supplier you buy from is committed to maintaining standards for quality and product safety during transport and storage.

- **Supplier Quality Assessment**: Implementing a systematic process to check all fish shipments that arrive on your doorstep for smell, texture, and other factors.

- **Measurement Systems Analysis**: Knowing how accurate, precise, and reliable the thermometer in your walk-in freezer, where you will store the fish, is. There's a big difference between a $5 refrigerator thermometer you pick up at the dollar store, and a $400 industrial thermometer that is more likely to detect small changes and last longer.

- **Chain of Custody**: Knowing when (and how long) a piece of fish, a food that requires consistent refrigeration, has been in and out of temperature control. Knowing where a piece of fish has been on its journey to your restaurant.

- **The Ingredient Journey**: Being able to trace the transport and processing of a piece of fish as it arrives, is cleaned and prepared, is cooked, and is plated and delivered to the customer who will make a determination of the meal's quality. Quality assurance at each of these steps helps the kitchen workers detect issues before they reach the customer.

- **Quality Assessment**: Implementing a systematic process to gather data about the state and characteristics of the fish as it is transformed from raw ingredient to prepared meal.

CONTEXT

To determine a plan of action, evidence must be examined for a particular business context and by one or more data literate people who are trained to recognize when that evidence can be used.

- **Relevance**: Is this evidence related to our decision process or business outcome?

- **Triangulation**: If the evidence is subjective or anecdotal, is there agreement between multiple measures?

- **Variation**: Do we have enough evidence gathered over time to distinguish between normal, expected variation and variation that indicates a shift in our process?

- **Risk Lens**: How dangerous it would be to use this data to make an incorrect decision?

- **Power Differentials**: How likely is it that our evidence is biased by power differentials (e.g. someone is fearful of saying what they really think because of a manager)?

- **Literacy**: Who understands the integrity of this evidence and knows how the resulting analytics should be shared and visualized? Are the right people engaged in the decision process?

In the industrial kitchen analogy, the context relates to what data and information is *useful, relevant, and trustworthy* given a restaurant's unique goals and the needs of their customers.

For each decision making process, ask: Is this evidence useful for ensuring the quality or relevance of the observation? If it is subjective or anecdotal, do we have corroboration from at least two other independent sources (triangulation)? Do we have enough information about the *variation* inherent in this data or information to figure out whether we should pivot, or hold steady? The risk of treating the data as evidence should also be explored. How dangerous could it be if we end up using this evidence and the evidence turns out to be wrong? What are the consequences to people, and to other systems? Is it possible that this evidence is unreliable due to power differentials, or any other aspect of the psychology of relationships ? Finally, how certain are we that this evidence, and our interpretation, are legitimate and reliable?

ACTION

The reason we gather, curate, and interpret evidence within a context is to identify one or more **actions** that can be directed towards realizing a desired outcome. In his 2015 book *Creating the Data-Driven Organization*, Anderson explains the importance of connecting actions with outcomes, citing an Accenture report:

Accenture found that 58% of executives see 'outcome from data' as a key analytics challenge. 'Establishing the linkage between data collection and analysis on the one hand, and the actions and outcomes predicated by analytics is proving to be a more difficult task for many than data collection or data integration.' Moreover, they found that only 39% of execs found that the data they generate is 'relevant to the business strategy.' This is where every member of the analytics org has a role to play. Help embed analytics into the business processes, and help make it easy, clear, and repeatable with relevant data and metrics.'

There are two components of facilitated action: 1) surrounding yourself with other professionals and leaders who value a data-driven approach, and 2) selecting or hiring a "cabal for change". While it's easy to understand why like-minded colleagues are valuable, the second component is even more critical.

Don't waste your time "getting people on board." Rather than trying to persuade skeptics that a data-determined action is something they'd want to do, it's more powerful to "identify people who are already enthusiastic about the idea and want the transformation to succeed… when people see that something is working, they want to be involved, and they bring in others who can bring in others still… [to] tip the scales toward widespread change. (Satell 2023)

TALKING THE TALK WITHOUT WALKING THE WALK

When you're identifying your "cabal for change," be on the lookout for people who *claim* to value the data-driven mindset, but subtly resist learning or investing in rigorous data collection, processing, or interpretation. While they may have genuine, pure intentions, this behavior means they are prioritizing other factors (like speed, decision control, information control, or preserving comfortable habits) over objective evidence.

Professionals and executives who proclaim a data-driven mindset but do not practice it can be detected in several ways. They often exhibit contradictory behaviors. For example, they might voice support for data-based decision-making in meetings or public announcements, but continually push back on projects or initiatives designed to collect and use data more effectively.

Their objections can range from budget constraints, to doubting the relevance or necessity of the data being gathered, to encouraging others to accept subjective observations as if they were objective. They might prioritize speed over accuracy or integrity or argue that doing things the "right" way will take too long. The business doesn't have time for rigor, they'll say.

They may have a propensity to rely on anecdotal or personal experiences over objective analytics, even when such data is readily available and relevant. They might make decisions based on personal biases or preconceived notions, then selectively interpret or outright dismiss data that contradicts their personal views and predispositions. Alternatively, they could disrupt the efforts of others directly (for example, by not approving budgets) or indirectly (by downplaying the importance of tasks that data and AI team members value, like allocating time for cleaning data and managing metadata).

These behaviors collectively signal a gap between professed and practiced values related to a data-driven mindset. Here are some of the phrases you might hear at work that indicate a value mismatch. These phrases will often be accompanied by a power differential, or an appeal for you to *just trust the person saying it*.

Being aware of these red flags can help you detect gaps:

- "I just have a gut feeling about this."
- "This is how we've always done it."
- "I remember when we tried that and it didn't work out."
- "I heard from a reliable source that..."
- "Based on my experience..."
- "I just know our customers and this is what they want."
- "I've got twenty years of experience and I know what the data should say."
- "Do we really need all this data to make a decision?"
- "Just use the data we have. We don't need it to be clean."
- "This worked well at my previous company."
- "I've gotten better results from people and intuition."
- "The data might say that, but my instinct tells me otherwise."
- "That's not relevant."
- "I trust my team."

There is, though, a role for subjective, anecdotal information and intuition to play in data-driven decision making. If you hear the same information from multiple, disconnected sources, *none of whom* have the ability or the incentive to coordinate messaging, there may be objective truth embedded in their message. This heuristic can be particularly useful when you are trying to make more data-driven decisions about human performance.

THE BOTTOM LINE

To be data-driven means to illuminate as many of the unknowns as is possible (and practical) to be able to distinguish reality from illusion, preferably in advance. Data-driven intelligence means getting the right data, of the right quality, to the right people (or systems) at the right time. The secret to becoming data-driven is to **focus on people**: how they collect, share, and interpret evidence within a given business context, and how power dynamics influence their habits, work practices, and relationships for good or ill.

Bean (2022) agrees. "In this year's [NewVantage Partners] survey, 91.9% of executives cite cultural obstacles as the greatest barrier to becoming data driven. As noted, this is not a technology issue. It is a people challenge." To become data-driven, we need to build habits on three organizational levels: as individuals, as teams, and within C-suites. To become a data-driven person, build the habit of valuing and seeking out *evidence* and adopt the practice of continuously questioning the data and information around you. To become a data-driven team, help each other build those habits and sustain those practices. All you need to remember are three power questions. When presented with data, information, or subjective assertions, ask:

- What evidence is this based on?
- Is it good, solid evidence?
- How can we be certain about the quality of the evidence, given the context of the decision we want to make?

For an organization to be data-driven, the value of data-driven thinking *must* be modeled starting at the top and reinforced all the way through the organization's hierarchy. If even *one* leader with power tends to favor emotions or side with ego over objective truth, the ripple effects through the organization will be palpable. Surrounding yourself with teammates who also value the data-driven mindset can protect against friction, disappointment, and new job searches.

REFERENCES

Bean, R. (2022, February 24). Why Becoming a Data-Driven Organization Is So Hard. *Harvard Business Review*. Available from https://hbr.org/2022/02/why-becoming-a-data-driven-organization-is-so-hard

Kitson, A., Harvey, G., & McCormack, B. (1998). Enabling the implementation of evidence based practice: a conceptual framework. *BMJ Quality & Safety*, 7(3), 149-158.

Satell, G. (2023, May 11). To Implement Change, You Don't Need to Convince Everyone at Once. *Harvard Business Review*. Available from https://hbr.org/2023/05/to-implement-change-you-dont-need-to-convince-everyone-at-once

PART III:

ELEVATING ORGANIZATIONAL PERFORMANCE

THE REASON I AM SO INEFFICIENT

https://xkcd.com/1445/

CHAPTER 8

ANTICIPATE FRAGILITY

"She eyes me like a Pisces when I am weak."
-- Kurt Cobain of Nirvana in "Heart-Shaped Box"

Jessica, the CEO's executive assistant, walked from office to office asking each employee the same question. "Are you the owner of the green 2002 Chevrolet Tahoe in the parking lot?" There were two police officers close behind her. At this point, I wasn't aware of that key detail, even as I heard the exchanges as they moved door to door.

A few seconds later she poked her head into my office. "Yep, it's me," I said. "The Tahoe is mine." The cops rushed in, puffed up like macho peacocks, hands on guns... one on each side of my desk.

"We'd like to ask you some questions about your stolen car."

I'm pretty sure I started laughing, which is not the best way to react to officers of the law. "My *what?*"

"Can you tell us when you first came in contact with the aforementioned vehicle in the parking lot?" Sure, I told them... I bought it on September 9, 2004 on my way back from outpatient surgery in Virginia to my house in West Virginia. They didn't like this answer, and the taller cop pulled up a chair. He'd sit there for nearly two hours as the officers probed, in greater and greater detail, the case of the stolen car.

I bought the car in Virginia, but lived in West Virginia at the time. Two years later, the car and I moved to Virginia. Turns out... the West Virginia Department of Motor Vehicles *never shared my change-of-address data* with Virginia's Department of Motor Vehicles. So somewhere, somehow, my car was flagged as "stolen" in Virginia's database. Once the two year mark hit, a trigger in their system set off the investigation that culminated in this sweaty and tense police interrogation that ate up several hours of my workday.

After digging up reams of documentation and making tens of phone calls together *with the speaker on*, the gun-toting cops were finally satisfied: it was a data error, and in the eyes of the law I now *legitimately* owned the truck I'd purchased a few years prior. There would be no jail for me.

EXPECT FRAGILITY

While it may have been *difficult* for states to exchange vehicle data in the days of the early internet, I certainly never expected that their business processes would be so fragile that I'd get a personal visit from cops with guns... years later. We all have conscious and subconscious expectations of how products and processes will perform, ranging from the food we eat and the vehicles we drive to the objects all around us.

One ordinary Tuesday, I was mixing tea in a bowl I bought in the mountains outside Nagano, Japan. I must have breathed on it too hard, because it shattered into pieces without much handling. I put the fragments in a Ziploc bag, and promised myself I'd repair it one day, maybe even learn the traditional Japanese method for doing the repair: kintsugi. This art, where broken pottery is repaired by binding broken seams with gold or silver, is often cited as an example of the beauty inherent in imperfection. But there's a part of the story that's *always* left out: the fact that those delicate Japanese cups and bowls *break easily*.

While some objects and systems are fragile and easy to break, others are literally broken all the time. Many of these are complex systems that we rely on every day in our businesses and in our lives. Our data ecosystems, too, are to some degree broken *all the time*. As leaders of our organizations, it is our job to recognize that impeccable architecture and perfect performance is not necessarily our goal.

Instead, we need to build resilient complex business processes that don't *appear* to fail - because they work everywhere we *need* them to work, at the *times* when we need them to perform.

COMPLEX DISTRIBUTED SYSTEMS

Fortunately, many complex distributed systems are intentionally designed for redundancy and resilience. (Tanenbaum 2007) Here are some examples:

- **Transportation networks:** Systems such as highways, railways, and airways often experience breakdowns in the capacity and availability of various segments due to incidents, work zones, weather conditions, or multiple factors. While there is no agreed-upon reliability measure for a transportation network, many can function normally even with partial capacity reductions or many completely unavailable segments.

- **Power grids:** Electricity grids are intricate systems that deliver power to homes, businesses, and industries. They consist of numerous components like generators, transformers, transmission lines, and distribution networks. Power outages or blackouts are common as a result of equipment failures, storms, overloads, and even human errors.

- **Computer networks:** Networks that facilitate communications and data transfer, like the internet, can have broken components or points of failure and still function. Routers, switches, servers, or network cables can malfunction, causing interruptions in connectivity or data loss in some cases, but never all.

- **Manufacturing plants:** Industrial facilities, including factories and assembly lines, rely on multiple machines, robotic systems, conveyors, and complex production processes. Equipment breakdowns, mechanical failures, or software glitches can lead to disruptions in production and delays.

- **Financial systems:** Financial institutions and stock markets operate intricate systems that handle transactions, settlements, and information flow. These systems can experience failures, software bugs, cyber-attacks, or issues with data integrity, resulting in errors, trade failures, or system downtime.

- **Telecommunication networks:** Telecommunication networks encompass telephone systems, cellular networks, and satellite communication. Network congestion, equipment failures, or natural disasters can lead to dropped calls, poor signal quality, or disruptions in communication services.

Your company is *also* broken all the time. On any given day, people will be out sick, on vacation, or committing all-too-human errors. On any given day, you'll have a backlog of repair tickets, a stack of customer complaints to handle, and new work that needs to be planned and performed. In most of these cases, we build redundancies, queues, and prioritization into our workflows to protect against the "failure states" we expect.

CONFUSION IS WASTE

Most data management and governance processes share the same weakest link: **the confusion that arises from ambiguity and obfuscation**. Actually knowing what happens along the data's journey from disparate raw inputs all the way to the finished data products that drive insights can be surprisingly shrouded in mystery. This lack of clarity seems to be a universal characteristic of organizations that collect, manage, and analyze data.

This isn't surprising. Most companies rely on a data ecosystem that grew and evolved *accidentally* rather than intentionally. Software engineers, who were focused on building new features, enhancing existing features, and releasing apps, sometimes had to deal with the data that their apps produced. They became more proficient at loading data, transforming data, and making it accessible to business users. But storing and curating data systematically was, if anything, an afterthought. Instead of a cohesive, well-architected data infrastructure, this patchwork of databases, data warehouses, and data pipelines cobbled together over time.

Data teams are left with a fragmented and disorganized data ecosystem, difficult to navigate, maintain, and scale. Left to reconstruct incomplete or inconsistent mental models of how the business works, data teams spend inordinate time and effort just trying to understand what data exists, where it resides, how to access it, and what it could mean. This lack of a unified understanding can lead to inconsistencies, duplications, and gaps in the data, making it challenging to extract legitimate and valuable insights.

VISIBILITY ISN'T AUTOMATIC

A business unit leader dropped by my office one morning. "Hey, I need you to tell me how many new small business users our new auto-registration feature brought in last week."

It was the first time I'd even *heard* that a new feature was planned, but at least it wasn't an entirely new product that was being dropped on me. "OK," I said. "Can you share the specs for the new feature? In particular, we'll need to know how to distinguish new users that came through this channel from new users that have come through other channels."

"We don't have any specs," he said. "It's the same registration process as before. Can't you just *tell me* how many new small business users we got from it?"

I'll spare you the rest of the anguish: there was *no way at all* to distinguish between the two user groups, and *also* no way to figure out if they were a business user - let alone a small business. Unfortunately that didn't help the analytics team, since the business leader just expected they'd figure out how to get the numbers regardless of feasibility. While the analysts were able to help the software engineers implement the tracking over the next week, we'd already lost two weeks' worth of data due to lack of observability.

Product management teams play an essential role in defining and driving the success of a company's products. They set the product vision, identify strategic goals, and ensure that the product meets the needs of the business and its customers. They conduct market research, interpret customer feedback, and collaborate with engineering, design, and marketing teams to bring their product to life.

It's an intense, high-stress job and there's always tension between adding new features, maintaining existing features, and battling technical and data debt. Tight deadlines and budget constraints are the norm, making product roles not only challenging but critical to the organization's success. Because new features drive revenue opportunities, the pressure is often extreme... executives are leaning on you to deliver on time.

Too often, "on time delivery" means that the feature *basically* exists, but you might not be able to get metrics about events triggered by that feature. Even when data and analytics teams haven't been involved at all in planning or developing the feature, they can still be expected to magically monitor results that can't be detected. It's a recipe for bad feelings all around:

- **Product managers** get frustrated because they can't report the results they're being asked for in business meetings, and they look bad

- **Executives** get frustrated by the data team, who couldn't deliver critical business data to the product managers

- **Software engineers** get frustrated because now the product team is asking for additional work that they didn't ask for in the first place, disrupting current priorities and further delaying already-late features

- **Data engineers** get frustrated because software engineers don't document their changes

- **Everyone** ends up with more "unplanned" work that

disrupts timelines and makes them all look bad

In this all too common scenario, expectations are disrupted, schedules are violated, everyone scurries to add band-aids to a process, people get frustrated by each other, and relationships and reputations are ruptured. The only solution is to allocate time up front for all affected parties to collaborate, come to a shared understanding, and define the new feature *and* how it will be monitored. Lack of clarity and collaboration leads to waste, rework, and bad feelings.

LACK OF CLARITY CAN ALSO BE EXPENSIVE

In April 2022, online media outlet Vice revealed a controversial whistleblower report. Facebook, the social media giant that has collected terabytes of personal data on people for nearly two decades, *has no idea* how any of its data is being used. When you share your personally identifiable information, your photos, and your events, there's no way for the company to determine who has access to that information or if (or how) it's been used.

This is a serious accusation for a lot of different reasons. First and foremost, Facebook is an international company, required (in many jurisdictions) to know how the personal data it collects is used. The GDPR, the European Union's General Data Protection Regulation (GDPR) that took effect in May 2018, regulates consent to access a user's personal information, even if that information is as simplistic as preferences logging into a website. GDPR also protects a consumer's right to know when their data is being exchanged with another company, and their "right to be forgotten."

GDPR is the reason we see so many prompts on websites asking you to "accept all cookies" – the companies behind those websites are required to capture your *consent* in addition to your data, and be able to explain where your data is used. Compounding the problem was that Facebook *specifically told its users it had this information, and could explain where your data was used if you asked...* which sounded great until someone decided to formally ask. Policy statements, after all, only cost pennies to invent. (GDPR isn't the only regulation that many companies have to adhere to. The California Consumer Privacy Act, the CCPA, has similar aims.)

Violations of GDPR can come with a $20 million fine, so accusations like this can pose serious threats to the viability of a business. Just in the four years between 2018 and 2021, nearly a thousand companies received violations, including Amazon and Google. The UK clothing firm H&M was also required to pay a 35 million pound fine, for improperly storing recordings of meetings (where employees shared events and issues in their personal lives) without getting the employees consent. The lesson to Facebook and other companies was: don't store or process data without knowing how you plan to use it.

You may already be thinking "but don't *most* companies store data without having a plan for how to use it?" and the answer is yes, and that's part of the problem. The material in the Vice article was based on a leaked internal document acknowledging the serious issues with data management and control inside Facebook, not just unfounded accusations. "Even Facebook's own engineers admit that they are struggling to make sense and keep track of where user data goes once it's inside Facebook's systems, according to the document. This problem inside Facebook is known as data lineage." (Franceschi-Bicchierai, 2022)

Data lineage is the key. For the past two decades, as companies have focused on data as a fixed asset, many have neglected to center their strategies around how value from data is generated. This value emerges as flowing streams of raw data become clean data, as clean data is assembled into data products, and as data products are consumed and interpreted to become insights.

WHY IS LINEAGE SO HARD TO GET?

Tracing data lineage to articulate every one of the processing steps as multiple raw data inputs are transformed, cleaned, and used to generate meaningful data products is *not* trivial. Why?

1. **Data ecosystems are cobbled together from many products**. In 2024, there were over 2000 startups providing products to make data acquisition, transformation, and processing easier in some way. Each of these systems captures metadata in different ways, complicating the ability to access it.

2. **Custom software components** may be in place to "glue" processes together, or as bespoke components where products were not purchased. These systems also capture and share metadata in unique ways.

3. **Security controls can obscure processing steps**. There's no guarantee that you'll be able to "peek into" any of the systems that capture or process data. Protection against cyberattacks is typically a higher priority than visibility and understanding.

4. **Inconsistent semantics**. Not every system will model core business processes in the same way, making it hard to uniformly track even common objects like Orders or Tickets across their entire lifecycle.

5. **Jargon**. Some off-the-shelf products do a great job probing the lineage of data - at the least, providing an excellent high-level picture of what's happening. But these systems are sensitive to the ways software engineers name fields, tables, and data objects... which is not always logical or intelligible.

Despite the challenges to visibility posed by purchased products, it's important to capture lineage in a way that data flows can be deciphered. Most data engineers will only spend 24 to 36 months at a company, and the metadata and mental models they develop in order to do their jobs has immense value. Without capturing and sharing lineage, institutional memory will be challenged, and people will spend lots of time trying to figure out why design decisions were made.

Don't expect managers to stop buying products to reduce the complexity. Managers also have to convince *their* managers of their value as an employee. Purchasing and implementing software products is an easy way to demonstrate that you've added value (whether or not you've added *real* value). In addition, there's an emotional payoff to signing a check: as a manager, if you've allocated a budget to solve a problem and then *use it*, you'll feel like you've solved the problem emotionally as soon as that payment is issued.

The increase in complexity *isn't* something a manager typically loses sleep over. After all, as a budget holder, it's relatively easy to throw more people and more positions at a problem. Unfortunately this is the status quo in software management, data management, and other engineering fields.

CHAOS & ENTROPY INCREASE COMPLEXITY

The chaos of complexity emerges because people are *rewarded* for adding it. The narrative of chaos *always serves someone* and for some purpose. Dysfunction forces power differentials, giving some people more power *than* others, and sometimes more power *over* others.   Typically, chaos benefits those who are already in power, because it helps leaders maintain control by keeping followers reactive and off balance.

Data is also subject to *entropy*. As you move forward in time, the degree of disorder in your data always increases. Documentation gets out of date, people forget the details of what they're working on after they move to work on something else, and turnover means that institutional knowledge about your data is often at risk.

Even the media that data is stored on becomes inaccessible or physically compromised over time. (How many old floppy disks or Atari cartridges are usable today?) Leaving things "the way they are" without maintenance or governance degrades quality over time, enhancing the potential for chaos.

As a result, software (and the data supporting it) tends to take on the structural characteristics of the organization that produced it. Known as Conway's Law, this pattern can be seen across many industries. (Tripp et al., 2018) Software and data architecture also encapsulates the dysfunction and chaos between the people that produced it, for good or ill. Chaotic and incomprehensible data can often be traced to the *power differentials* and *incentives* driving the people who conceived it and created it.

*"As students graduate with degrees that have effectively prepared them for Generative AI, we'll see a gap emerge in the workforce. **The most AI-fluent workers will be the** most junior, the individual contributors, the* **organizationally disempowered.**

Higher education needs to teach skills in coalition building, systems thinking, building consensus, and building expertise in managing up, down, and laterally."
– Dr. Cory Knobel, CEO of Research at Work

When there is a lack of clear communication, collaboration, and shared goals between these stakeholders, the data ecosystem (and the data it produces) becomes fragmented, inconsistent, and difficult to navigate. Underlying tensions and conflicts between people manifest themselves in data silos, inconsistent definitions, and poor documentation. Because no workplace is a psychosocial utopia, all data ecosystems will be imperfect – but you can use that knowledge to your advantage by accepting it as a premise.

For example, be selective about how much effort time and effort to invest into planning and preparation, strategically choosing the approach that will result in the lowest possible cost or loss overall. After all, in the words of Harry Truman, *imperfect action is better than perfect action* (except for when imperfect action leads to greater losses overall). (Radziwill 2019)

THE BOTTOM LINE

Every system, including the data ecosystem your company works within, is *some degree of broken, all the time.* When we architect and operate systems that provide data, information, and insights to others, we should anticipate fragility. This includes unavoidable failures, imperfect understanding, and fractured communication. The larger a system gets, the more broken stuff there will be at any given time. As organizations grow, the more likely it will be for someone to be in (or recovering from) a "failure state." By treating each other with empathy and respect, we can minimize the sting of those failure states.

> *"Research tells us that **negative interactions have as much as five times the impact of positive ones**. Removing even a few negative relationships can make a significant difference in your overall microstress level."*
> *– Rob Cross & Karen Dillon in The Microstress Effect*

Whether you're responsible for a business process or the data it produces, focus on *getting the most important parts right the most often*:

☑ Data the most people need most often.
☑ Data that supports *high value decisions*.
☑ Data used to mitigate or reduce important risks.

Additionally, focus your efforts on the "Vital Few" metrics for each department or functional area (3-5 KPIs). Ask yourself what constitutes "Minimum Viable Governance" - that is, the *minimum* actions you need to take to ensure that your data *stays* in the state you expect.

Embrace the reality that no system is perfect, and prioritize the time and effort on the most critical aspects of your data ecosystem. By focusing on the vital few metrics, supporting high-value decisions, and implementing minimum viable governance, you can navigate the challenges of a complex evolving data landscape, subject to the power dynamics and incentives that real people invariably respond to.

REFERENCES

Tanenbaum, A. S. (2007). Distributed systems: principles and paradigms. Pearson, Upper Saddle River, NJ.

Franceschi-Bicchierai, L. (2022, April 26). Facebook Doesn't Know What It Does with Your Data, Or Where It Goes: Leaked Document. *Vice.* Available from https://www.vice.com/en/article/akvmke/facebook-doesnt-know-what-it-does-with-your-data-or-where-it-goes

Radziwill, N.M. (2019, March 2). Imperfect Action is Better than Perfect Action: What Harry Truman can Teach Us About Loss Functions. *Quality & Innovation.* Available from https://qualityandinnovation.com/2019/03/02/imperfect-action-is-better-than-perfect-inaction-what-harry-truman-can-teach-us-about-loss-functions-with-an-intro-to-ggplot/

Tripp, J., Saltz, J., & Turk, D. (2018). Thoughts on current and future research on agile and lean: ensuring relevance and rigor. Available from https://scholarspace.manoa.hawaii.edu/bitstreams/77b0c456-a564-474d-a4fe-89503ebb6687/download

CHAPTER 9

INFUSE DATA WITH POWER

"The idea, product, or data never speaks for itself.
It lives or dies on the story that you tell about it."
-- Michael Margolis, CEO of Storied

Losing $2B would be tragic for any company, but it's particularly tragic when a company is diligently *trying* to lean on data to make intelligent data-driven decisions. That's what happened when Walmart decided to declutter its aisles in 2009, after a customer survey *overwhelmingly* indicated that shoppers wanted a fresher, cleaner, more open in-store experience... like Target. (Popken 2011)

What went wrong? It turns out that while customers might *say* they want less clutter in stores like Walmart, and might actually desire it, less clutter doesn't translate to more sales. That "clutter" actually ends up fueling unplanned additions to the shopping cart and triggering impulse buys. When a company gathers information about customer satisfaction and preferences, it's usually motivated by a desire to tune products and services to their needs, driven by an underlying desire to increase revenue. But it's always essential to first consider the validity of your assumptions.

Walmart made two costly mistakes: first, they assumed that

giving customers what they *said* they wanted would increase revenue (and failed to experimentally seek evidence of the causal link between those two things). Second, their customer survey included a leading question: "Would you like Walmart to be less cluttered?" There is a universe of possibilities for actions Walmart could take to increase customer satisfaction in ways that would positively impact revenue, but Walmart assumed that the openness of the floorspace was the issue at hand. By phrasing the question the way they did, Walmart restricted that universe to one option: removing the "clutter" that was driving billions in revenue.

While it's useful to capture data like this, data only becomes *infused with power* when you can understand and effectively apply it in the context of a relevant, meaningful business problem. Acquiring data is *good*. Verifying that your data is good is *much better*. Ensuring that your strategy uses meaningful data to compel action gives you *leverage*. Deming's system of profound knowledge (see, for example, Deming 2005) reveals that to produce the leverage that will change culture through data, we have to address four elements: the *knowledge* that is produced, the *system* it is embedded within, the *psychology* of the people in that system, and the power of using *variation* to your advantage.

WHAT'S IN IT FOR ME?

First, you have to find ways to *extract* data from the brains, mouths, and fingers of the people who could provide it to you. For decades, the difficulty of getting customers or prospects to fill out surveys has been well established, in part because "people differ in what they consider to be a reward, a cost and whether a request is trustworthy." (Sammut et al., 2022) It can also be challenging to entice employees to consistently provide good data through applications and other software interfaces. People use software because they're *motivated to get their own work done*, not by a desire to store accurate, complete, consistent, and valid data that will grow in value as an asset for their organization over time (despite what many software and data people actively hope).

Social exchange. Is the effort worth your time? It's human nature to weigh the cost of an interaction against the benefits that could result from that interaction, according to social exchange theory. Consequently, people tend to be more willing to provide data when they feel they will personally benefit in some way. Will I get paid? Will I be contributing to a cause I believe in? Will this help someone I care about? Will this help someone whose success I'm invested in? Will this get me formal or informal recognition that's meaningful to me?

Data collection design. Since there's always a social cost of providing data, data collection mechanisms have to be designed so that contributing information is *simple, natural, immediate,* and *unblocked*. Ask for only what you need, avoid ambiguity or complexity, ask in the moment, and make sure your data collection process functions as intended. And while the unending need for simple and natural software interfaces is the reason there are so many user experience (UX) specialists, "system" doesn't necessarily need to mean software. Museums and art installations often struggle to get feedback from visitors, and have uncovered valuable insights about how to collect data using physical design.

Physical design. Data can be collected in creative ways by taking advantage of physical actions people naturally take in the normal course of engaging with a company or an institution. For example, one museum recognized that everyone was asked to return their entry badges upon exiting the building. Rather than just throwing them away, they recognized that they could use that physical action to collect data. The museum set up five receptacles, each labeled with a sad face or smiley face, and asked visitors to drop their badge in the bin that matched their experience of that day. Through this one act of creative physical design, the museum increased their response rate for a satisfaction survey from under 10% to nearly 100%. (Simon 2010)

Measurement systems alignment. Good design shouldn't just happen at the level of data collection, but also in how that data is structured, manipulated, cleaned, and used to generate new information. For example, at one company I advised, three departments disagreed on whether customers were satisfied... *or* not. I asked to look at their customer satisfaction data, and noticed curious similarities, differences, and patterns. Each department was measuring customer satisfaction in an entirely different way, and *none* of them were legitimately revealing how customers actually felt. We reengineered the measurement systems across those departments to make sure we were measuring the right things at the right times, *consistently*, and sharing data so that decisions could be aligned across all departments.

Perverse Incentives. One of the most insidious root causes of bad data is people. When incentives unintentionally produce exactly the opposite behaviors or outcomes they were designed to bring about, they are called "perverse incentives". These incentives can lead individuals to impede rather than advance objectives. When it comes to data quality, perverse incentives are not uncommon. A company might incentivize its data entry clerks based on the number of records they input in a given timeframe, hoping to increase productivity. However, this might lead them to race forward without adequately checking for accuracy. Similarly, when data is crowdsourced, if contributors are rewarded for the number of entries they make (rather than the accuracy of those entries) an influx of inaccurate or duplicate data is sure to occur.

WHEN GOOD INTENTIONS BRING DATA DEBT

Sales executives are notorious for doing *anything* that needs to be done to get a deal closed, especially when they have to reach their monthly targets. This often has consequences for data quality. As one example, after the financial crisis of 2008, Wells Fargo instituted the "Eight is Great" program that encouraged every representative to upsell an extra eight accounts for each bank customer. Fearing layoffs, sales representatives did what they do best: they figured out how to sell the new accounts. Over the next several years, "the incentive resulted in disaster... Wells Fargo employees created more than 1.5 million unauthorized deposit accounts, and at least 500,000 unauthorized credit card applications." (Tarallo, 2018)

This program of perverse incentives actually created bigger problems on much longer timescales. In 2016, Wells Fargo was fined $185M by the U.S. Government. By 2018, the company had to respond to $2.7B in lawsuits, both civil and criminal. Today, there are probably Wells Fargo employees who are *still* dealing with the duplicate data and ghost accounts enthusiastically created by thousands of salespeople for years. Because the cost of remediation and lost time could easily also be in the billions, this case illustrates how the power of ordinary actions can lead to unintended consequences.

LEVERAGING THE LATENT POWER OF ORDINARY ACTIONS

Optical Character Recognition (OCR) technology is much more sophisticated and advanced today than anyone might have imagined upon its genesis in 1914. Originally conceived as a way to automatically convert written text to telegraph messages, it evolved into a utility to search microfilm by the 1930s, patented, and purchased by IBM. In the 1970s, renowned computer scientist Ray Kurzweil decided to enhance it further, expanding its ability to recognize different fonts and convert text to speech. (Asif et al., 2014)

Despite the revolutionary nature of the technology, OCR never quite achieved a state of technical nirvana. By the early 2000s, the digitization process for documents and books was still imperfect, recognizing only a fifth of the words in historical documents where the ink had faded or the pages had weathered. In contrast, two humans independently deciphering a word and comparing their results could achieve more than 99% accuracy. But "human transcribers are expensive, so only documents of extreme importance are manually transcribed." (von Ahn et al., 2008) But digitizing books and documents opens up access to those works not only to humans, but also to train AI. There had to be a better (and cheaper) way to make historical documents and archives more accessible through the internet.

Luis von Ahn, a computer science professor at Carnegie Mellon, thought so too. Applying social exchange theory, he imagined scenarios where humans might be willing to decipher digitally transcribed words and phrases for free (and maybe even enjoy doing it). First, he recognized that people would gladly decipher characters in an image if doing so got them something they wanted, like access to something else on the web (like the CAPTCHA challenge-response tests that were ubiquitous online in the 2000s.) Second, he imagined that they might contribute their effort if the digitization was somehow made into a game.

At that time, users were typing more than 100 million CAPTCHAs a day, an effort that von Ahn realized was largely going to waste because it wasn't capturing any new information... all of the CAPTCHAs presented to users had known answers. What if, he thought, the user was asked to input *two* words into their CAPTCHA, where one was known and the second was an unknown word or phrase captured from a historical document? By keeping track of results between multiple users, he could simulate two or more human transcribers comparing their results, and achieve 99% or greater accuracy while transforming all of that human effort into valuable outcomes.

His innovation, called reCAPTCHA, quickly became the web standard. It was acquired by Google in 2009, and powered the digitization of hundreds of thousands of records and many Google Books.

While this approach to transforming non-value-adding work to value-adding was praised by many, it was criticized by some who accused Google of relying on unpaid labor to do its work. (Harris 2015) The reCAPTCHA utility was turned off by Google in 2018, superseded by "invisible CAPTCHA" that assesses whether a user is a human or a bot without direct interaction. Even considering the social and political issues that emerged around the reCAPTCHA project, it's still an excellent example of how to creatively engage a crowd to generate high quality sources of data and information.

"CAPTCHAs constitute a viable mechanism to harness large amounts of human mental effort. After exactly 1 year of running the system, humans had solved more than 1.2 billion [re]CAPTCHAs, amounting to over 440 million suspicious words correctly deciphered.

Assuming 100,000 words per book (400 pages, 250 words per page), this is equivalent to over 17,600 books manually transcribed (about 25% of the words in each book are marked as suspicious by our algorithm)... [As of 2008, the] rate of transcription currently exceeds 4 million suspicious words per day, which is equivalent to about 160 books per day.

Achieving this rate via conventional 'key and verify' means (without aid from OCR, so every word in a text would be typed) would require a workforce of more than 1500 people deciphering words 40 hours per week (assuming an average rate of 60 words per minute)." (von Ahn et al, 2008)

PROXY DATA

Sometimes it's difficult (or even impossible) to directly measure something you'd *like* to measure. In cases like this, indirect evidence that *can* be directly measured, or *proxy data*, can be valuable.

Use of proxy data is a familiar technique for many disciplines. Climate scientists infer climatological patterns by examining measurements like sediment, tree rings, ice cores, and even historical documents for hints about weather conditions and key weather events (see, for example, Martin-Puertas et al., 2014). Specialists in Environmental, Social, and Governance (ESG) reporting know that sometimes proxy data can be the only way to estimate greenhouse gas emissions, and others report the data quality metric of completeness as a proxy for "the emphasis each company gives to these themes." (Brounen et al., 2021) At the height of the pandemic, scientists working in public health looked to proxy data observable at wastewater treatment plants, in an effort to trace the regional spread of the contagion. (McManus et al., 2023)

One of the biggest threats to the validity of information you collect is the risk of *not actually* measuring or assessing the thing you *think* you are. This risk is especially pronounced if you're working with proxy data. Inputs that look and feel trustworthy may (in fact) be anything but, so you'll have to dig deeper to understand how and where data originates, and how it becomes the measurements you'll use to support your decisions. Sometimes, that understanding will be hidden from you by others, obscured by the human desire to preserve existing power structures or motivated by the drive to subvert them. Here are some real examples:

- **You sell a SaaS software product** that has been installed and configured for your client, a 500 employee environmental management firm. What you don't know is that your company measures customer satisfaction by sending a survey by email to the client's head of procurement, who's never used your product, asking him how satisfied their organization is with the compliance tools you have provided. He gives you 10 out of 10 because he had a great contracting experience with you, likes your CEO, and wants your company to succeed. Meanwhile, the real users remain unhappy, and the Customer Success reps lose a little more power to enact meaningful change day after day.

- **A leadership team** is reviewing individual performance and customer satisfaction data to make strategic decisions about workforce capability and capacity. One of the leaders shares that they've categorized their team members into three groups: high performers, average performers, and people who need improvement. The two people who consistently receive the lowest objective performance and satisfaction scores are listed as high performers. How is this possible? To maintain power and bypass the risk of losing headcount, the leader has subjectively assigned these characterizations, independent of any objective performance or satisfaction data, to take advantage of her colleagues' assumptions about how the categories were assigned.

- **A business unit at a large multinational bank** needs to use a particular table in a production database to make a critical decision each month. They do not know which IT team manages this table, but they do know that the table changes suddenly and without warning a couple times a month. They make a copy of the production table and set up a schedule to replicate it. Over the course of a decade, this process plays out a multitude of times, leading to nearly two thousand untraceable (and unmaintainable) replicas, and extensive use of proxy data that may or may not align with an authoritative source.

In each of these cases, a proxy is chosen because the business needs information to make a decision, but the phenomenon of interest is not directly observable or there is risk associated with using the direct measurements. In the first case, people are doing what they think is right, and producing data to support decisions that need to be made. They may feel like they don't have the time to verify how customer satisfaction is measured, or may assume that since their department has been using that measurement for years, it must be valid. In the second case, the leader is attempting to provide the management team with data that supports their desire. The motivation is not nefarious, but instead, is an attempt to reduce this leader's future stress. In the third case, the business unit is trying to avoid the future consequences of using data they do not control.

In most cases, people are not *trying* to create bad data, just trying to get a job done. A lack of attention to where data is coming from, how it is being transformed into usable information, and how it is being interpreted and used can impede progress over time.

While a lack of transparency can ultimately lead an organization into unhelpful situations and disasters on all scales, there's one tool that can be used to mitigate the risk: triangulation.

TRIANGULATION

In July 2023, a mother and daughter were traveling home to Denver from a lacrosse tournament in Baltimore. Fearing the loss of the daughter's expensive equipment, they affixed an electronic airtag to the luggage to track it in case they became separated from their cargo. While airlines track luggage by tagging it with barcodes, this method can only report where the bag was last scanned, not its current location. An airtag, in contrast, is a beacon that only reports its current location.

When the mother contacted the airline to report that the baggage didn't arrive in Denver as expected, the customer service agent reported that the equipment would arrive later that night. When it didn't, the mother called back. "Your bag is in Baltimore," they reported. But she knew this was inaccurate, because the airtag was sending a signal from Chicago. This discrepancy could occur if the barcoded sticker became detached from the bag (somewhat likely), if the airtag fell off the bag (less likely), or if someone forgot to scan the bag or had affixed the wrong label to it at check-in (most likely).

The last scenario is what happened in this case: the agent at check-in placed the wrong barcoded sticker on the lacrosse equipment. But armed with the airtag data (and sufficient resources to make an extra trip), the mother returned to Chicago where she found the bag exactly where the airtag said it would be. This example illustrates how using *triangulation* can help your organization unlock the power of good information. Using this approach, you consider the *agreement or disagreement* between related values rather than just a single measurement.

THE BOTTOM LINE

Data becomes infused with power when it is produced by known, robust processes and paired with business context that provides *shared meaning*. Your power to assess the present and predict the future is conditional on the data you use to make those judgments. The ability to *get* data is good, but the ability to *verify* your data is good is much better. Leverage emerges from strategies that require meaningful data to compel action, recognizing the role that human nature invariably plays.

"You keep using that word.
I do not think it means what you think it means."
-- Inigo Montoya in The Princess Bride (1987)

While we need good information to make decisions, plenty of people have good reasons to give us *no data* or *bad data*. We can use psychology to collect and validate better inputs, keeping a human in loop as necessary.

To do this, we need to consider social exchange theory (making sure people have a reason to provide good data), data collection design (providing simple, natural, immediate, and unblocked interfaces to ease the process), physical design (using natural actions to collect data), measurement systems alignment (verifying that metrics are consistent across people and departments), and perverse incentives (making sure people aren't accidentally rewarded for holding back information or enthusiastically providing too much of it).

In all cases, you'll need to answer these questions:

- **Engagement:** How do you entice people to contribute good data and information?

- **Governance:** How do you entice people to engage with data production and curation processes, continually generating higher value data assets over time? How can you convince executives that clean data is not optional, but critical?

- **Triangulation:** How can you design triangulation into data collection and validation processes to protect against human error, system errors, and power dynamics?

Changing culture with data is an *evolutionary* process. First, take steps to get *good* data and information consistently. Make sure everyone shares an understanding of what input data means and the processes used to get the information needed to make decisions.

Triangulate wherever possible to get a feel for how variation impacts raw data and the impact of this variation on accuracy. Once the business can make better, faster decisions, the energy (and willpower) for the workforce to sustain healthy data collection and validation processes grows.

REFERENCES

Asif, A. M. A. M., Hannan, S. A., Perwej, Y., & Vithalrao, M. A. (2014). An overview and applications of optical character recognition. *Int. J. Adv. Res. Sci. Eng*, 3(7), 261-274.

Brounen, D., Marcato, G., & Opt Veld, H. (2021). Pricing ESG equity ratings and underlying data in listed real estate securities. *Sustainability*, 13(4), 2037.

Buckley, J. (2023, August 30). The airline said her bag was lost, but her

tracker said otherwise. So she flew to get it. *CNN Blog.* Available from
https://www.yahoo.com/lifestyle/airline-said-her-bag-lost-082404332.html

Deming, W. E. (2005). A system of profound knowledge. In W. Edwards
Deming: Critical Evaluations in Business and Management, 1, 89.

Harris, D. L. (2015, January 23). Massachusetts woman's lawsuit accuses
Google of using free labor to transcribe books, newspapers. *Boston
Business Journal.* Archived from the original on April 28, 2015. Retrieved
September 4, 2015.

Martin-Puertas, C., Brauer, A., Wulf, S., Ott, F., Lauterbach, S., & Dulski, P.
(2014). Annual proxy data from Lago Grande di Monticchio (southern
Italy) between 76 and 112 ka: new chronological constraints and insights
on abrupt climatic oscillations. *Climate of the Past*, 10(6), 2099-2114.

McManus, O., Christiansen, L. E., Nauta, M., Krogsgaard, L. W.,
Bahrenscheer, N. S., von Kappelgaard, L., ... & Ethelberg, S. (2023).
Predicting COVID-19 Incidence Using Wastewater Surveillance Data,
Denmark, October 2021–June 2022. Emerging Infectious Diseases, 29(8),
1589.

Popken, B. (2011, April 18). Walmart Declutters Aisles Per Customers'
Request, Then Loses $1.85 Billion In Sales. *Consumerist.* Available from
https://consumerist.com/2011/04/18/walmart-declutters-aisles-per-customer-request-then-loses-185-billion-in-sales/

Sammut, R., Griscti, O., & Norman, I. J. (2021). Strategies to improve
response rates to web surveys: a literature review. *International Journal
of Nursing Studies*, 123, 104058.

Simon, N. (2010). The participatory museum. Museum 2.0, Santa Cruz,
CA.

Tarallo, M. (2018, February 28). Paved with Good Intentions: How
Employee Incentives Can Go Awry. Society for Human Resources
Management. Available from
https://www.shrm.org/ResourcesAndTools/hr-topics/organizational-

and-employee-development/Pages/Paved-with-Good-Intentions-How-Employee-Incentives-Can-Go-Awry.aspx

Von Ahn, L., Maurer, B., McMillen, C., Abraham, D., & Blum, M. (2008). ReCAPTCHA: Human-based character recognition via web security measures. *Science*, 321(5895), 1465-1468.

CHAPTER 10

CREATE BELIEFS THAT INSPIRE

"If you want something from an audience, you give blood to their fantasies. It's the ultimate hustle."
- Marlon Brando

On January 21, 2022, a marketing team scrambled to send an important message to 400,000 of a company's entire roster of 4.265 million registered users. (Son, 2023) Time was of the essence, because the U.S. Free Application for Federal Student Aid (FAFSA) form had just been released. The company knew that most of its registered users would be completing the FAFSA in February, and they wanted *as many of them as possible* to use their *very* convenient service... which would make the form easier to fill out, and more likely to yield the desired loan amounts. This was the first campaign planned for that purpose.

Finally, the message was ready to go out, and the emails started towards their destinations. The marketing team excitedly braced itself for the next phase of the customer journey: converting those leads into paying customers.

The joy would be short lived.

Within minutes, the team knew there was a problem. *Most of the emails were bouncing back, undelivered,* indicating a problem somewhere. Was there a mail server down at headquarters? Was

Amazon Web Services (AWS) down? Did someone accidentally send the batch of emails to the data on the test server? Some quick triage by the engineers revealed that everything was, unfortunately, operating perfectly nominally. *Still, only 2 out of every 10 emails were reliably getting to a recipient's inbox.* This wasn't good.

Someone quickly submitted a work ticket to the helpdesk, marking it highest priority so it would be escalated immediately to the data team. Soon, the verdict emerged: there was a data quality problem, and it was irreparable. Many of the email addresses (like asdugnsdf@gmail.com) appeared to have been randomly generated, and didn't actually correspond to the registered user in the company's database, or even any person at all.

It didn't take long for the matter to reach the executive team. Everyone could feel it... *heads were about to roll.*

SIX MONTHS EARLIER

By the summer of 2021, young entrepreneur Charlie Javice was ready to take a big leap. Her tiny 15-person startup, Frank, was now four years old. It had been getting national attention since its earliest days, landing her a spot on the Forbes 30 Under 30 in 2016.

Frank's web site provided information for high school students and their parents about scholarships, college courses, and navigating the financial aid process. It provided an unparalleled experience for helping people get started with their college plans, and made it easier for enrolled students to maintain the financial support they needed to complete their degrees. And by making the FAFSA form easier to submit, a notoriously painful rite of passage for nearly every student, the company claimed it had helped "millions of students obtain billions of dollars of student aid" by early 2021. It was a remarkable accomplishment, made only more notable because she wouldn't even turn 30 until 2023.

It was time to find a buyer for the small company, and finding businesses who wanted to hear the pitch from such a high-profile young entrepreneur wasn't difficult. Charlie approached the financial giant JPMorgan Chase (JPMC), who wanted to expand its market for financial services to college-age students, and a meeting was set. Her pitch was perfect: In addition to 4.25 million registered users, "expressly defining a 'user' as an individual who created a Frank account by entering a first name, last name, email, and phone number on Frank's website" (X, 2023) the website had significant ongoing engagement, with over 35 million visitors since its inception.

Acquiring customers can be *expensive*... and marketing departments exist to make it happen more easily. When a company wants to achieve growth targets in a new market, it can be difficult to find *leads*, let alone the kind of *pre-qualified leads* that Frank's service was attracting with ease. While it took $1.3 million to get the word out in the company's first two years, marketing spend had decreased year over year, and Frank only planned to spend about $50K on marketing in 2021. The two graphs that showed decrease in marketing spend compared to the consistent increase in registered users could only be described as magical. This suggested that there were clear network effects and word-of-mouth referrals.

Compared to the typical cost of $300-3000 to acquire each lead for this target market, JPMC would only pay $41 for each *qualified* lead if they bought Frank. As a bonus, they would get a fully functioning website that could keep generating leads in perpetuity.

JPMC is a huge company, and they had gone through the acquisition process plenty of times before encountering Frank. They knew it would be important to independently check the integrity of the claims in Charlie Javice's pitch, and the due diligence process began in earnest. The investment team visited the acquisition data room, a website that contained financials, accounting statements, and auditing statements. They held more than one synchronous session where the prospective investors posted questions to the founders, and got answers from Javice.

On July 14, 2021, JPMC submitted a notice of intent to acquire the startup. At $175 million dollars, the 4.25 million customers they would obtain was undeniably a bargain.

MEASURE TWICE, CUT ONCE

On August 1, 2021, JPMC's Head of Corporate Development reached out for "two critical confirmatory due diligence requests." Basically, to close the deal, *they needed to prove that the 4.25 million users were real.* JPMC asked Frank to provide metrics from profiling the data about completeness (how many entries were completely populated with first name, last name, date of birth, phone number, address, *and* email address). They asked how many customer records were *partially* complete. They also asked for a breakdown of completeness by each of those six fields. They asked how many customer records were unique.

In addition to providing the summary data, JPMC wanted to see examples of customer records. Javice agreed to provide them, but noted that email and home street addresses would be recoded as unique keys, not as the original values. She couldn't do any more than that, she said. She was concerned about data privacy, and didn't want to share the rest of the records directly with JPMC. The firm engaged a third-party vendor to act as an intermediary, believing that it would help preserve privacy while allowing the parties to complete the due diligence process and prevent the acquisition deal from stalling.

Just four days later, Frank provided 4,265,085 million customer records to the vendor. The deal was ratified on August 8, and closed on September 14. Javice and her co-founder Olivier Amar were able to cash out several million dollars each. They were also offered full time positions at JPMC, and lucrative bonuses.

A SIDE QUEST ABOUT DATA QUALITY

Completeness is only one of many data quality dimensions that can be used to evaluate whether an individual field, or an observation that consists of multiple fields, is "good." Other dimensions include timeliness (the data is available when you need it), validity (the data is represented in the expected format), consistency (the data matches records stored elsewhere), and accuracy (whether the data represents reality).

To close the deal, JPMC asked Frank to describe the completeness and uniqueness of the customer data. By inquiring about completeness, the firm was checking to ensure that there was enough information in each customer record to identify that customer and use it effectively as a lead. For example, a record that only had an email address (but was missing everything else) might be minimally viable, but how can you really target your marketing if you don't know what state or province someone lives in? Whether someone will have in state, out of state, or international student status is critical to know in the world of federal student aid.

JPMC also expressed interest in uniqueness. Are each of the

customer records *different* from the others, or are there fewer actual registered users than registered user records? To get an accurate count of customers, we shouldn't be double (or triple) counting. By checking on uniqueness, JPMC could explore whether Frank's customer database had issues with duplication that might obscure the true number of registered users.

Here's the catch: it's possible to have customer records that are unique and complete, but not usable at all as leads. At the field level, I can report phone numbers that are formatted properly (validity), where the country code matches the country of origin for the customer (consistency), and where the phone number will actually connect me with a real person, but not the real person I am expecting. The phone number may appear to be perfect where data quality is concerned, but still not be an accurate means of contacting the customer I need to contact. This is why "fitness for purpose" is such an important concept in data quality: can a particular person or system *do what it needs to do* with this data?

What JPMC was really interested in was the data quality dimension of accuracy. Does each of these customer records represent a *real person that we have enough information to contact*? Unfortunately, accuracy is one of the most difficult data quality dimensions to examine.

THINGS ARE NOT ALWAYS AS THEY SEEM

On the surface, JPMC's August 1 request for metrics was straightforward and simple. Behind the scenes, the Frank team had to scramble. They only had 293,192 *real* registered users, despite what they had presented during the due diligence meetings, and within the acquisition data room. Javice, however, was not deterred: this *tiny* discrepancy *would not* stand between her and a $175 million dollar exit.

She and co-founder Amar launched a two-pronged attack: he would work with a third party data source provider to *purchase* 4.2 million more customer records. She would work with Frank's director of engineering to *generate* 4.2 million more records. "Not comfortable, the engineer asked Javice and Amar whether the request was legal. In response, Javice sought to assure the engineer that she was not requesting that the engineer engage in illegal conduct. The Frank engineer was not persuaded and declined to participate in the scheme, and instead said that he would only provide Javice with Frank's actual list of customer accounts: fewer than 300,000 customer accounts as of July 31, 2021." (JPMorgan Chase Bank N.A. vs Javice and Omar, 2022)

While this was disappointing to her, it was not a complete roadblock. Charlie Javice had one more avenue to explore to quickly get the synthetic data she needed.

THE VALUE OF SYNTHETIC DATA

There are valid and necessary reasons to fabricate data. Most of those reasons relate to anonymization of personal information, and providing data to software engineers and quality assurance specialists for testing. After all, although you could conceivably test online banking software with real user accounts, real transactions, or real ledger balances... not only would that increase risk, but it would also violate the rights of those real users.

"Synthetic data... are indispensable when access to actual data is restricted. Notably, under most privacy regulations, e.g., EU's General Data Protection Regulation (GDPR) 'repurposing' of personal data is prohibited without explicit consent. This complicates sharing of any actual personal data with third parties who are responsible for software development and testing." (Soltana et al., 2017)

According to Assefa et al. (2020) who work in artificial intelligence for the financial services industry, "data sharing within different lines of [a financial services] business as well as outside of the organization is severely limited. It is therefore critical to investigate methods for synthesizing financial datasets that follow the same properties of the real data while respecting the need for privacy of the parties involved in a particular dataset." Creating datasets that maintain the same structural and statistical properties of real datasets is absolutely essential for supporting software development, identifying new features for training AI and machine learning models, and testing those models prior to release.

Even though synthetic data doesn't describe real entities or characteristics, and can't in many cases be considered *accurate*, it's important to make sure it's valid, consistent, complete, unique, and (sometimes) precise, to ensure that there is no loss of information content. For physical data like inputs to weather forecasts, synthetic data does need to be somewhat accurate, in the sense that it must accurately portray real-world conditions. (Gupta, 2014)

Expertly crafting synthetic data that is "fit for purpose" requires significant skill and expertise. As a result, Charlie Javice decided to engage a data science professor at a university in New York City to create synthetic data for Frank, as a backup, in case Amar's efforts didn't yield the desired results.

Email communications reviewed by the court, between Javice and the data science professor, suggest that the professor probably wasn't aware of the acquisition discussions proceeding in the background. He or she likely assumed that Frank was working on a new AI model, and needed to generate a large set of unique customer records for testing. In this case, the data science professor may regret making those assumptions for all eternity.

THE HOUSE OF CARDS

The deal went through. Large sums of money were exchanged. And the ruse would be effective until January 21, 2021, when the core Frank team had to transfer *real* customer records to the new team at JPMC for its first marketing campaign. At this point, JPMC was the rightful owner of the records, so there was no way out for Charlie and her co-conspirator. It's unclear, at this point, whether Javice and Amar knew their house of cards had started to crumble.

First, the emails began to bounce. With 28% send completion, this campaign was already notably different from other email campaigns, which averaged 99% send completion. Only 1.1% of the delivered emails were even opened. As the JPMC marketing team looked into it more, they started noticing curious anomalies. "I can also confirm that there are 1,048,575 records, plus the header row. One observation – 1,048,576 (total including header) is the maximum # of rows allowed in Microsoft Excel – can we be sure that this is just a coincidence, or maybe there is some data truncation after that row?" (JPMorgan Chase Bank N.A. vs Javice and Omar, 2022)

The discrepancies were concerning enough that JPMC immediately revisited the terms of the Frank acquisition, as well as the information gathered during discovery and due diligence. The conclusion was stark: an entire team of investors had been moved by the power of data - in particular, two charts that showed the compelling growth of registered users under decreasing marketing spend. They thought Frank was a unicorn because of these high multiple returns; what they didn't realize was that Frank was a unicorn because its results were entirely fictitious.

In December 2022, JPMC sued the founders for fraud. "JPMC paid $175 million for what it believed was a business deeply engaged with the college-aged market segment with 4.265 million customers; instead, it received a business with fewer than 300,000 customers… [which] materially damaged JPMC in an amount to be proven at trial, but not less than $175 million." (JPMorgan Chase Bank N.A. vs Javice and Omar, 2022)

Javice's attorney didn't agree, and argued that JPMC's court case is retaliation for Javice's actions as a whistleblower after the company failed to pay her $28 million. (Reuters, 2023)

TURNING ENERGY INTO MATTER

Einstein told us that energy and matter are one and the same, and one can be converted into the other. The most straightforward example of this is that burning fuel produces energy, whether that fuel is gasoline or the body mass you're trying to burn at the gym. Instruments like the Large Hadron Collider (LHC) in Geneva, Switzerland exist because it's possible to create matter by smashing beams of light into each other at high enough speeds (although scientists are still working on making that practical).

The *most powerful* way to turn energy into matter is to translate inspiration and ideas (energy) to create new realities (matter). Entrepreneurs are masters of inspiration. They have an idea, and through their own belief in the power of that idea becoming real, they build stories that inspire other people. When they can inspire people and organizations who have resources (like funding) to back their ideas, the energy turns into matter and other things *that* matter: new value, new capabilities, new companies, and new benefits for the customers those companies serve.

In the case of JPMC's acquisition of Frank, when Javice shared her inspiring graphs, she released the tremendous energy of inspiration among the investment team. They saw an amazing deal, and the possibilities that her lead generation engine made real. And while that's the *point* of pitches and demos in general, the dynamics can become litigious when the terms of a promise are violated. (Vago, 2023) She fooled us, so she's the villain, court filings suggest. But how much responsibility should *we* take for allowing the power of data to inspire us, and compel us to action?

THE BOTTOM LINE

Data catalyzes belief, and belief releases the energy of inspiration. The energy of inspiration is the ultimate holy grail – because *that* can be converted into the matter that matters the most to entrepreneurs and investors: money. When data causes people to believe so *unfailingly* in the revenue generating power of an idea, companies (like JPMC, in the Charlie Javice story) are compelled to invest.

The investors are trusting not in physical reality, but in the reality that they have *personally constructed* based on the data, analytics, and insights they interpret themselves, the reality they have been *led to believe by the data*, and the reality they have been *led to believe by the person (or system) delivering the data*. Sometimes this is perfectly truthful, because physical reality is close enough to what the data indicates, or will catch up in time.

More often, we're swayed by enticing stories that may or may not be connected to the data used to tell them, building the excitement that eventually turns to hype. Other times, we're swayed by the power and influence of the storyteller, or the power dynamics between us and them. Leaders and storytellers can use data purely as a blunt instrument of their power, a mechanism to obscure, impress, and manipulate. More power is unleashed, however, when data is used as a compass to build shared understanding, rally group inspiration, and create new realities together.

REFERENCES

Assefa, S. A., Dervovic, D., Mahfouz, M., Tillman, R. E., Reddy, P., & Veloso, M. (2020, October). Generating synthetic data in finance: opportunities, challenges and pitfalls. In Proceedings of the First ACM International Conference on AI in Finance (pp. 1-8).

JPMorgan Chase Bank N.A. v. Charlie Javice and Olivier Amar, Case 1:22-cv-01621-MN. (U.S. District Court Delaware 2022). https://s3.documentcloud.org/documents/23571709/jp-morgan-v-javice-1.pdf

Reuters. (2023, January 12). JPMorgan shuts down financial planning website Frank after suing founder. Available from https://www.reuters.com/legal/jpmorgan-shuts-down-financial-planning-website-frank-after-suing-founder-2023-01-12/

Soltana, G., Sabetzadeh, M., & Briand, L. C. (2017, October). Synthetic data generation for statistical testing. In 2017 32nd IEEE/ACM International Conference on Automated Software Engineering (ASE) (pp. 872-882). IEEE.

Son, H. (2023, January 12). JPMorgan shutters website it paid $175 million for, accuses founder of inventing millions of accounts. *CNBC Blog.* Available from https://www.cnbc.com/2023/01/12/jpmorgan-chase-shutters-student-financial-aid-website-frank.html

Vago, A. (2023, January 12). So, We Crucified Elizabeth Holmes. To What End? Holmes wasn't the real fraud. We were. We still are… Available from https://attilavago.medium.com/so-we-crucified-elizabeth-holmes-to-what-end-84795929f6fb

CHAPTER 11

RAISE THE BAR

"[Chefs at Michelin-starred restaurants] teach you how to operate on a level you didn't know you could operate at."
-- Carmy Berzatto, restaurant owner in The Bear (TV show)

Whether you win or lose a game, a good coach *always* gathers the team to reflect on the experience. What went well? What went wrong? Are we improving in the ways we *want* to? Are we falling short? What other ways can we improve, and what ways *should* we improve? The coach's job is to ask probing, emotional questions, sometimes rhetorical, to get you to figure out *where your heart is* and where your heart *needs to be*.

The coach helps you and your teammates seek out and identify the problems that are inhibiting your performance as an individual, and the problems that arise in your interactions and relationships with others. The coach brings you and your colleagues together to reaffirm where you want to go together, and how you can iterate and adjust so you can get there in a way that is ultimately rewarding.

The coach helps you define, pursue, and achieve a quality culture. If the effort (which will take months, and sometimes years) is successful, you'll win games... and achieve personal wins along the way.

THE BEAR

TV series *The Bear* (2023) focuses on the lives of 8 people who work together in a restaurant. In addition to the interpersonal drama, the show's excellent cinematography helps viewers feel the panic, the chaos, the always-on tension of playing an active role in an industrial kitchen. I've never worked in a restaurant, so I had little to relate to. And to be honest, Season 1 kind of stressed me out with its fast pace and constant agitation.

The show starts as Carmy, the main character, returns to Chicago after the unexpected suicide of his brother Mikey, who owned a gritty neighborhood restaurant called "The Original Beef of Chicagoland" – a long-time community favorite. Mikey has left the restaurant to Carmy, who is an award-winning chef from a Michelin-starred restaurant in New York, entrusting him to take up the helm at the head of the family business. While the family is proud of his accomplishments and happy he's returned, there are clearly tense family dynamics and a lingering sense of betrayal that he had left Chicago while they remained stuck there.

POWER DIFFERENTIALS ARISE

As soon as Carmy arrives at The Beef, there's a palpable power differential: While Carmy is in charge, he's new. The entire rest of the staff has been there for months already, maybe years, and have habits and routines of their own. They're accustomed to doing their own thing, figuring things out as they go along, and bristle at Carmy's attempt to manage.

On his own, Carmy has brought in an unpaid intern, a talented young chef named Sydney who's trained at some of the most reputable places in town and, admiring Carmy's reputation, wants to work with him... even if it's at the sandwich shop her father's been going to for years, and not a fine dining establishment.

Carmy and Sydney are accustomed to an entirely different mode of operation than the old timers at The Beef. His quality and performance standards are much, much higher; Sydney has joined him because she *shares* those standards. The others have lower expectations of themselves and their restaurant, and don't particularly have a reason to change that.

The performance differential sets up a cultural rift: the previous staff, in particular "Cousin Richie" (who's not actually a cousin), get the sense that Carmy and Sydney think they're better than everyone else (even though they just want the staff to learn and grow). The tension is particularly high with Tina, a long-time restaurant worker who's not particularly enthusiastic about change, but had been committed to brother Mikey's establishment and wanted it to succeed.

Soon, they notice Carmy doing strange things: being particular about his (and their) methods for preparing and cooking dishes; cleaning all sorts of things with a toothbrush, including the floor; and engaging in rigorous routines, many for outcomes they didn't see the value in.

"It's about consistency," he says, "You can't operate at a higher level without it." His experiences training under world class chefs has opened his eyes to what is possible, and he aspires to the excellence that he observed.

THE RESISTANCE OF SELF-INTEREST

Humans are programmed to survive, even in work environments. Survival means preserving enough power and authority to do several things, including get your own work done, maintain the relationships that make that job possible or impossible, and keep the paychecks coming.

> *"In a world of **competing separate selves** seeking to maximize rational self-interest, some authority is needed to suppress this interest-seeking for the sake of the common good. The discipline it imposes… is from the individual's point of view a kind of suffering.*
>
> *People must be made to do what they don't want to do, and to refrain from doing what they want to do. Internalized, **it is a war against the self**, a fight against desire or pleasure, a battle of biology against will."*
> *(Eisenstein 2022)*

Carmy's reappearance in Chicago was bound to lead to resistance. First, the restaurant has been legally given to him, and he's the new owner. The staff knows that they will be getting direction from an unfamiliar boss, and they're accustomed to Mikey's values and management style. While they may have trusted his brother, they don't have a basis (yet) to trust Carmy. The team is also a little reluctant to make themselves vulnerable because they perceive him as an outsider, someone who left the familiar tough Chicago environment in favor of the fancy work of upscale New York. They create an illusion of who they think Carmy is, and it allows them to project all of their fears in one direction.

But *why*, you might ask, would the workers resist changes that will reduce chaos, that will bring the restaurant smoother operations, and that will level them up in terms of performance? Why is there so much fear and doubt, and so little vulnerability, openness, or communication? It's because it's (biologically) easier to stay fearful than it is to make a change.

Markus (1983) asked this exact question four decades ago, when she explored why workers rejected new software systems even when those systems brought clear and demonstrable benefits, improving the business and personal workflows. She discovered that, holding all other factors equal, *people will always resist change*. It takes cognitive energy to shift habits and practices, and the threshold to suppress change is surprisingly low.

When people resist, she explains, there are three potential sources. First, the person resisting *might just be a stubborn agent of obstruction.* No matter what you do, or how compelling the change is, they're not going to buy in. Markus explains that you have to either force those people to change, for example through penalties or incentives, or remove them from your organization. Alternatively, their resistance might be coming from technology – if the tools and processes people are expected to start using *just don't work*, they're not going to adopt the change and start using the new process or system.

Finally, the resistance might be coming not from individuals but from the *interactions between them* that create or reinforce power differentials. Before deciding that someone is a jerk, explore the possibility that the change may exacerbate someone's feelings of powerlessness. If a change can make one person or group more powerful at the expense of another, by recognizing this you have the opportunity to design that inequity out of the system up front.

When you're assessing readiness for change, it can help to pinpoint the pockets of resistance, recognizing that you *will* encounter them. Fortunately, most of the resistance that Markus and partners observed was from shifts in power, not because people are trying to be difficult. However, don't adopt a strategy of trying to convince the naysayers. Research shows *that doesn't work.* It's better to build momentum by engaging people who already believe in the change. (Satell 2019)

PERFORMANCE GAPS MOTIVATE CHANGE

Carmy *sees* the performance gap between his team and himself, but also sees the performance gap between his own level of performance and *where he aspires to be*. **He meets them where they are**, because he knows they're not emotionally ready for breakthrough improvements, and The Beef isn't exactly a candidate for Michelin stars. He models the desired behaviors, and never relents: each day, every day, in his interactions with every person, he calls out performance gaps and sets the expectation that *he won't compromise on quality*. Meanwhile, they get to observe Sydney's higher standards, and how Carmy responds – and builds on – her work.

Gradually, and with much pain and friction, the team develops practices that are *acceptable enough* for Carmy, at least **for the time being**. He finds he's got bigger problems: the financial state of the business wasn't as stable as he was originally led to believe, and the restaurant is struggling. They try experimenting: new recipes, new menu items, and "take out" – but each potential new path fails. He finds out that he's deep in debt to the Mob, and even if he could pay it off, the restaurant is unlikely to survive.

Tension rises – and in a moment of exhaustion, Carmy berates Sydney for minor issues, reminiscent of the abusive treatment he received from his primary mentor. Sydney's not going to put up with abuse of any kind. She quits, leaving Carmy with even more work to do to keep the restaurant afloat.

While Season 1 culminates with Carmy finding hundreds of thousands of dollars stashed in tomato sauce cans that he can use to repay his debt to the Mob, there's still not enough liquidity for him to keep The Beef in operation. But the team has an idea: they're ready for the next step, and they want to do it together. Sydney returns at just the right moment to rejoin the crew.

Together, they hang a sign on the door announcing that "The Bear" is coming soon.

BUILDING NEW HABITS AND PRACTICES

Season 2 highlights **transformation**: building habits and practices that reflect a new understanding of quality standards, and a dedication to excellence and continuous improvement. Marcus, the pastry chef, heads to Copenhagen to study under a master. Tina heads to chef school. Cantankerous Richie (who, it appears, feels like he's so battle-worn and experienced *he belligerently doesn't need any chef school*) is assigned to one of Chicago's best restaurants (called "Ever" – it actually exists) for shadowing.

Richie resists, complains, lashes out... and even considers quitting. After a few days of rudely resisting his mentors' attempts to level him up, he decides to accept his "punishment" and put up with the menial tasks he feels they are asking him to focus on. He's been a chef for years. Why are they having him spend so much time *polishing forks*?

In a moment reminiscent of the "wax on, wax off" scene in 1984 film *The Karate Kid*, Richie has an epiphany. He *sees just how good it feels to embrace quality in a new way.* He finds his best self, and becomes a warm, attentive colleague, tuning into a talent of connecting with people that we hadn't yet seen (but Carmy was clearly aware of, and waiting for its resurrection).

DISCIPLINE CATALYZES AN INNER SHIFT

Meanwhile, *the building itself transforms* in ways that mirror the psychological transformations: walls are torn down, and walls fall down on their own (forcing a vulnerability that the characters aren't quite ready for). Mold pours out of the ceiling, and all over Richie. The fire suppression system has been tampered with and is no longer functional, and the team has to reverse the damage to get the license to operate. Floors are shined; cozy new lighting is installed. Tables are tightened. A gift arrives in the mail from Denmark, and Marcus hangs it – an "Every Second Counts" sign – under the clock in the kitchen to remind everyone of their shared strategy for banding together in times of crisis to remember their goals.

The team manages to band together for a "Friends and Family" opening night that ends up being... mostly successful. Carmy gets locked in the walk-in refrigerator when the handle breaks off, clearly some karma for his resistance to handing off the "call fridge guy" task to *literally anyone else for three months*. In a fit of shame and self-flagellation he vocally expresses his regret about prioritizing a new girlfriend over his restaurant, but she's been listening to his diatribe the whole time...

So we're well set up for another season, where the characters realize that even though they've been through training, they don't have things figured out just yet, and building a quality culture takes lots of time and a ton of shared dedication. This is probably the *best* series with a quality theme that I've ever seen, and certainly the best of any restaurant show I can think of (I'm comparing it to *Alice*, *SpongeBob*, and the short-lived sequel to Three's Company called *Three's a Crowd*).

I'm looking forward to Season 3 of The Bear. The characters will surely get to know the new quality standards more intimately, and recognize, likely in painful ways, that **excellence is a journey, not a destination**.

DATA, STRATEGY, CULTURE & POWER

The Bear shows us how data, strategy, culture and power are all prominent, interconnected, and intertwined - particularly when an organization begins a transformation through quality. It also shows us that transformation is a process. It's not quick, and it's not something that magically happens without pain and adjustment from many people.

Season 2 brought a new emphasis on **data**. First, we see Carmy and Sydney taste testing new potential dishes, relying on each other to provide contrast to each other's personal observations. During the restaurant's physical renovation, the team installed a kanban system to track the work required to deliver a particular dish, and designated a person to optimize the schedule and direct the activities of the rest of the kitchen staff. They hung a clock, prominently, in a central location on the kitchen wall. They set up timers, challenging themselves to complete parts of the food preparation process in just a few minutes. They started gathering customer feedback.

The **strategy**, describing what they could (and would) do with the data, was also consciously shifted. Every strategy has, at a minimum, three elements: an articulation of where you're going (goals), an explanation of how you'll try to get there (actions), and an idea of how you'll know when you got there (metrics). Carmy's strategy in Season 2 is to focus on the unique value he knows he can provide to his community through fine dining, leveraging the skills and intentions he shares with Sydney to drive a more sustainable business model with higher margins.

While the **culture** of The Beef wasn't quality driven, the strategy for The Bear was completely driven by a new commitment to quality and growth. Carmy invested in opportunities for each person to see and feel higher quality standards, and recognized that the process was just as likely to help people improve as it was to chase them away. Ultimately, they find common ground in the pursuit of their new quality standards by reminding each other that "Every Second Counts" - the sign that hangs just below the central kitchen clock.

Despite the early **power** differentials, the interpersonal discomfort it revealed, and the inner discomfort that each person as they realized their world was definitely about to change (whether they wanted it to or not), Carmy ultimately helped the team achieve the first stage of their transformation. Not only has each person found and learned how to tap into their inner sources of power, but they now have practice working together to leverage collective power. The experience of a satisfying opening night unleashes the inspiration to more fully embrace their roles as essential workers in a fine dining establishment.

WHAT IS A DATA-DRIVEN QUALITY CULTURE?

In a data-driven organization, decisions are made by collecting, analyzing, and interpreting data instead of relying on intuition, anecdotes, or personal experiences. By seeking to understand patterns, trends, and insights, strategic decisions and tactical adjustments can be informed by objective evidence. A data-driven mindset acknowledges the importance of objective data and values the insights derived from it, even when those insights are uncomfortable or reveal problems that need to be solved.

A quality culture is characterized by a shared belief and commitment among all members of the organization to prioritize, maintain, and continually improve quality. Quality isn't the responsibility of a specific department dedicated to quality, but instead, is the responsibility of everyone in the organization. This mindset promotes accountability, a focus on customer satisfaction, and a constant pursuit of excellence. "When quality is defined culturally... the focus of attention shifts to the effects of an organization's values, attitudes, and expectations reflecting its quality principles." (Cameron & Sine, 1999)

Embedded a data-driven approach within a quality culture can be a powerful accelerator for achieving excellence and sustainability in any organization. This way, decisions related to performance and improvement are not made solely on the basis of experience or intuition, but are always backed by quantifiable information. Taking this approach ensures that quality improvements are measurable, repeatable, and scalable.

Quality takes time but pays off many times over. An objective, systematic, and trusted approach to achieving desired performance levels while remaining committed to continuous improvement leads to greater customer satisfaction, improved reputation, and ultimately, increased competitiveness.

THE BOTTOM LINE

A data-driven culture of quality values *objective evidence* over intuition, anecdotes, or personal experiences in a quest to continually achieve high levels of quality. Through expectation gaps, performance gaps, and the less visible gaps created by uncomfortable power differentials, we come to understand what changes are required to level up performance.

If you're committed to quality, you will seek to understand what "good" means, searching *beyond the bounds of your own knowledge* for a higher external standard. You will work to objectively achieve those standards. You seek out data to honestly appraise your performance, gathering perspectives and interpretations from others. You know the risks of self-delusion and overconfidence. As you engage with others, you model how to objectively create, use, and interpret data. You hold others to the same high standards *you* hold for yourself.

The biggest threats to a quality culture are the inability to distinguish what "good" looks and feels like, a lack of humility (and thinking that you already know, and that there's nothing left to learn), and a willingness to cut corners. The ultimate goal is to operate effortlessly, together, at a level that you didn't know you could operate on before.

Change is rough on the brain, even when people *want* to transform. To achieve these new levels of performance, you'll have to build new habits and patterns – not just on your own, but also in relationship with other people. This isn't easy. Old habits are hard to break because people are literally fighting their own *biology*, regardless of their intention, because any change requires spending cognitive and emotional energy. In addition, learning new habits and practices is a lot easier than *unlearning* old ones, regardless of how early or late you are in your career.

Ultimately, every achievement comes not from a lone genius, but from networks of people working together over time. And "working together" doesn't always mean working together frictionlessly, or easily. *Every* person is susceptible to day to day variation: circumstances, situations, and *moods* change, and struggles with family members or friends can even impact your ability to show up as a productive collaborator. People you don't get along with *at all* might work with *each other* splendidly. The way we *see* our friends and colleagues treated by managers and executives will impact how we act at work, and how guardedly we respond to leaders in the future. Interpersonal relationships with coworkers and bosses form, change, end, and are destroyed as the cycle continues.

Data (and by extension, AI) can be powerful tools for growth or harm. Rather than pretending like irrationality, self-interest, and self-preservation don't exist, we need to account for these immutable forces in our companies as we plan and carry out data strategies and embed AI into business functions.

This book is a call to action: *it's up to us* to surface the often invisible ways data and AI reshapes power dynamics and our lived experiences at work. It's essential that we recognize data and AI not as mere tools, but as *active forces* in consciously building the social fabric of organizations.

REFERENCES

Cameron, K., & Sine, W. (1999). A framework for organizational quality culture. *Quality Management Journal*, 6(4), 7-25.

Eisenstein, C. (2022, December 11). Handfuls of Dust and Splinters of Bone, Part 2. *Charles Eisenstein Newsletter*.

Markus, M. L. (1983). Power, politics, and MIS implementation. *Communications of the ACM*, 26(6), 430-444.

Satell, G. (2019). Cascades: How to Create a Movement that Drives Transformational Change. McGraw Hill Professional.

AFTERWORD

Between 70-90% of *all* digital transformation initiatives, which includes data, analytics, and artificial intelligence (AI) projects, fail. *Why isn't anyone getting it right?* I reflected on this question for nearly a decade only to discover that engineer and quality guru W. Edwards Deming had the answer years ago.

Deming's grit, to me, is inspirational. He waited until well after retirement age to see his revolutionary work appreciated in his own country. One of his contributions was the **System of Profound Knowledge (SPK)**, shared in a presentation he gave at the age of 90. It marked cumulative learnings from his high-impact career educating Japanese and American executives about quality, operations, and data-driven management.

The goal of this book was to translate Deming's thinking into stories that would make his work relevant for data, analytics, AI and quality professionals in the 2020s and beyond. SPK for data and AI means:

- Ensuring transparency to reveal how **knowledge** is produced,
- Understanding the **systems** that data flows reflect,
- Probing the **psychology** of the people who influence and engage with data producing systems to uncover and address how power dynamics might shift with data, and
- Applying techniques like triangulation to harness the power of **variation** to your advantage.

Empowered with this understanding, you'll be able to detect power differentials and use them to build more effective *power-sensitive strategies* for generating and using data, analytics, and AI more easily.

ABOUT THE AUTHOR

Dr. Nicole M. Radziwill is an internationally recognized expert in data management, digital transformation, and Quality 4.0. She has helped 35+ CEOs and Chief Data & Analytics/AI build and execute effective, empowering data & AI strategies since 2018. She draws from more than 20 years' experience as a senior and executive level leader in roles including VP Quality, SVP, Chief Data Officer, Chief Data Scientist, plus a decade as a tenured Associate Professor of Data Science and Production Systems at James Madison University (JMU).

As Chief Strategy Officer of Qzuku, she empowers high-growth startups and Fortune 1000 clients to leverage AI and data through power-sensitive Data/AI strategies. Understanding that the success of any AI initiative relies on the strength of the team behind it, she helps clients cultivate high-performing and inclusive Data/AI teams that value collaboration, innovation, and continuous learning.

Dr. Radziwill also works directly with clients as an interim Chief Data & AI Officer and executive data scientist, organizing AI product management, building models, and supporting go-to-market efforts. She is the architect of the intelligent agents (powered by machine learning) driving the powerful TeamX (team-x.ai) platform, serves on the Advisory Board for the Great Expectations data quality framework providing go-to-market support, and partners with acadalyst.com and client companies to help MS and PhD candidates be more productive performers in industry.

Nicole is an elected Academician in the International Academy of Quality (IAQ) and a Fellow of the American Society for Quality (ASQ). She has a PhD in Quality Systems and an MBA. Previous books include *Connected, Intelligent, Automated: The Definitive Guide to Digital Transformation and Quality 4.0 (2020)* and *Statistics (The Easier Way) With R (2019)*, which is used in over 30 universities around the world.

She is also a Burner and can often be found at the 9 o'clock Post Office.

$$\frac{\text{PRECISE}}{\text{NUMBER}} + \frac{\text{PRECISE}}{\text{NUMBER}} = \text{SLIGHTLY LESS PRECISE NUMBER}$$

$$\frac{\text{PRECISE}}{\text{NUMBER}} \times \frac{\text{PRECISE}}{\text{NUMBER}} = \text{SLIGHTLY LESS PRECISE NUMBER}$$

$$\frac{\text{PRECISE}}{\text{NUMBER}} + \text{GARBAGE} = \text{GARBAGE}$$

$$\frac{\text{PRECISE}}{\text{NUMBER}} \times \text{GARBAGE} = \text{GARBAGE}$$

$$\sqrt{\text{GARBAGE}} = \text{LESS BAD GARBAGE}$$

$$(\text{GARBAGE})^2 = \text{WORSE GARBAGE}$$

$$\frac{1}{N} \sum \left(\begin{array}{c} \text{N PIECES OF STATISTICALLY} \\ \text{INDEPENDENT GARBAGE} \end{array} \right) = \text{BETTER GARBAGE}$$

$$\left(\frac{\text{PRECISE}}{\text{NUMBER}} \right)^{\text{GARBAGE}} = \text{MUCH WORSE GARBAGE}$$

$$\text{GARBAGE} - \text{GARBAGE} = \text{MUCH WORSE GARBAGE}$$

$$\frac{\text{PRECISE NUMBER}}{\text{GARBAGE} - \text{GARBAGE}} = \text{MUCH WORSE GARBAGE, POSSIBLE DIVISION BY ZERO}$$

$$\text{GARBAGE} \times 0 = \text{PRECISE NUMBER}$$

https://xkcd.com/2295/

ACKNOWLEDGEMENTS

There's no way to *completely* capture the rich tapestry of people I've learned from, chatted with, and drawn inspiration from over the years to result in the insights captured in this book. While I've learned as much from the negative examples around me as the positive (and maybe more!) there are several of my colleagues whose positive demonstrations of "people first leadership" or insightful reflections on power and data have had an impact on how ideas in this book formed and evolved.

While this list is not exhaustive, almost certainly impacted by recency bias, and alphabetical to keep it easy, I'd like to thank *at least* the following people: Rajesh Anandan, Morgan Benton, Brent Brewington, Cedric Chen, T. Scott Clendaniel, Marcia Conner, Rob Cross, Beth Cudney, John Cutler, Cara Dailey, Alex Radziwill Debarba, Joseph DeFeo, Ray Flynn, Graham Freeman, Abe Gong, John Hagel, Nicola Jaine, Saul Kaplan, Ray Kanani, Cory Knobel, Jami Kovach, Valdis Krebs, Michael Margolis, Danielle Navarro, Jacqueline Nolis, Tom Peters, Corrie Pitzer, Howard Rheingold, Allison Sagraves, Greg Satell, Art Schechtman, Amanda Slavin, Harsh Thakkar, Siva Vaidhyanathan, Mark Vicente, Ergest Xheblati, Dave Zeeman, all of the executive leaders and Chief Data Officers I've waxed philosophical with about pain points, and everyone in the International Academy of Quality (IAQ) with whom I continue to enjoy stimulating and rewarding conversations on a regular basis.

Usher.
I can thank you

Made in United States
North Haven, CT
18 July 2024

54949258R00111